REVEALING wisdom on the walk

an anthology PLUS
compiled by

lori l. dixon Ed.S.

Copyright © 2023 Lori L. Dixon

ISBN: 978-1-64396-334-1

All rights reserved. No part of this book may be reproduced or transmitted in any form or by any means, electronic or mechanical, including photocopying, recording or by any information storage and retrieval system without written permission of the publisher, except for the inclusion of brief quotations in a review.

Book design by Callie Revell, callierevell.com

Published by LLD Legacy Publishing

Printed in the United States of America

Scripture quotations marked "ASV" are taken from the American Standard Version Bible (Public Domain).

Scripture quotations marked "AMP" are taken from the Amplified® Bible, Copyright © 1954, 1958, 1962, 1964, 1965, 1987 by The Lockman Foundation. Used by permission. www.Lockman.org

Scripture quotations marked "ESV" are from the ESV Bible® (The Holy Bible, English Standard Version®), copyright © 2001 by Crossway Bibles, a publishing ministry of Good News Publishers. Used by permission. All rights reserved. www.crossway.org

Scripture quotations marked "KJV" are taken from the Holy Bible, King James Version (Public Domain).

Scripture quotations marked (NIV) are taken from the Holy Bible, New International Version®, NIV®. Copyright © 1973, 1978, 1984 by Biblica, Inc.™ Used by permission of Zondervan. All rights reserved worldwide. www.zondervan.com

Scripture quotations marked "NKJV" are taken from the New King James Version. Copyright © 1982 by Thomas Nelson, Inc. Used by permission. All rights reserved. Bible text from the New King James Version® is not to be reproduced in copies or otherwise by any means except as permitted in writing by Thomas Nelson, Inc., Attn: Bible Rights and Permissions, P.O. Box 141000, Nashville, TN 37214-1000. www.nelsonbibles.com

Scripture quotations marked (NLT) are taken from the Holy Bible, New Living Translation, copyright © 1996, 2004, 2007 by Tyndale House Foundation. Used by permission of Tyndale House Publishers, Inc., Carol Stream, Illinois 60188. All rights reserved. www.newlivingtranslation.com, http://www.tyndale.com

Scripture quotations marked "MSG" or "The Message" are taken from The Message. Copyright 1993, 1994, 1995, 1996, 2000, 2001, 2002. Used by permission of NavPress Publishing Group. www.navpress.com

Scripture quotations marked "TPT" are from The Passion Translation®. Copyright © 2017, 2018 by Passion & Fire Ministries, Inc. Used by permission. All rights reserved. ThePassionTranslation.com.

This book is dedicated to **my mom**, for so many stories are being told within this book from my life with you, Dad, and Susie. Your joy and laughter still ring in my heart and spirit. I thank you for the experiences we shared. Whether they are of significant loss or great abundance, we did them as a family.
I was honored to call you my mom and dad.

This book is also dedicated to my husband and life partner, **Art Dixon**. He continues to be my rock and greatest supporter, and no matter what life throws our way, we find the steps to take together and walk in faithfulness and hope in the wisdom of our walk with God.

And for the first time, I dedicate this book to the "littles" and "not-so-littles" in our life, **Hannah**, **Catie**, **Lilly**, **Clark**, and **Logan**. The times we have spent with you bring Grandpa and me (Nana) joy, balance, and true bliss. No matter what the walk of life brings to us, we are always here for you in the love of the Lord and the truth He shares in our lives. We pray you will walk in a relationship with Him and learn the true purpose and mission He has instilled. Remember how much you are loved and accepted!

Finally, this book is dedicated to our **Father**, **Daddy**, **God**, for nothing would make sense without Him. For Jesus, his son, who has prepared a way forward for each of us and the great comforter and speaker into our lives, the Holy Spirit, for whom we feel blessed to hear your words and guidance daily. Thank you!

"Trust in the Lord with all your heart, and do not lean on your own understanding. In all your ways acknowledge him, and he will make straight your paths. Be not wise in your own eyes; fear the Lord, and turn away from evil." Proverbs 3:5-7 ESV

Gratitude Glory Connect Growth Wisdom Warrior Balance Seek Faithfulness Joy Compassion Soar Intentional Bliss Family Love Surrender Dream Big Patience Reveal Shine Rooted

appreciation

Words cannot express the work of so many hands that have gone into this book and the women who have brought their stories to life to ripple the words and experiences of God in their lives.

To the twelve women sharing your twelve stories of transformation, wisdom, faith, hope, and LOVE with the world: May each of you, who have become sisters in Christ, use this as a stepping stone in building not only your missions and assignments for God but how those stones fit into the structure of the Kingdom of God as it is created today on earth. "As Earth as it is in Heaven…" So glad God chose YOU!

To the team of *Wisdom on the Walk*: Jordan Mitchell, Shae Stewart, Callie Revell, Jordan and Kim Gosnell—I thank you for bringing your faith, heart, and talents to God in this beautiful outpouring of experiences for the healing of many. You all are the foundation of the Kingdom! Love you all!

To Stephanie Vasquez for her artistic work and support to make the chapter ideas come alive. Way to go, girl!

To our production team of Lance and Eric… you are always at your best when you can be behind the "curtain" of a creation. Thank you for blessing us with your talents and support for putting our books into the world. YOU ROCK!

To my family for always being supportive of my writing attire, my schedule of intensity, and my talents being used for God's mission and purpose.

To my "new" sister, Jody Glass, for inspiring me to walk further in my Spirit-filled talent and purpose for God, the divine dad, and His son, our Lord. Thank you for the leading and training you continue to do in my life so I may affect others further in their journey to healing in God. Thank you for writing within the chapter of my birth and life, which God was so ready for it to be told … me … A little reluctant yet, listening.

To our Father God—We are blessed to serve you and your mission for this earth. Thank you!

> "Write down the revelation and make it plain on tablets so that a hear and may run with it. For the revelation awaits an appointed time; it speaks of the end and will it prove false. Though he linger, wait for him; he will certainly come and will not delay." Habakkuk 2:5

contents

Introduction 9
Lori L. Dixon, Ed.S.

Wisdom In the Meantime 15
Krista Medlock

Dream Big 29
Lori L. Dixon, Ed.S.

Rooted and Established In Christ 39
Jackie Davis

Compassionate Compass of Life 53
Lori L. Dixon, Ed.S.

Kingdom Seeker 65
Shae Stewart

Listen Now to a Love Song 81
Lori L. Dixon, Ed.S.

The Glory Steps 95
Lulite Ejigu

Patience On the Walk 113
Lori L. Dixon, Ed.S.

Open Heart 121
Judy Cochrane

Balance and Bliss 137
Lori L. Dixon, Ed.S.

The Walk of the Warrior Spirit.. 151
Deanna Blair

Walk of Growth 167
Stephanie Vasquez

You Can't Hug a Palm Tree 179
Lori L. Dixon, Ed.S.

The Walk of What If to I Wonder... 189
Becky Dozeman, MSW, LMSW

I've Got the Joy!... 209
Lori L. Dixon, Ed.S.

Is This My Life?.. 223
Molly Brown

What's In Your Cup?... 235
Lori L. Dixon, Ed.S

Shine, Don't Shrink.. 243
Irum Rashid-Jones

Wisdom of Gratitude 257
Lori L. Dixon, Ed.S.

Intentional Connections 275
Allison Byrd-Haley

Wisdom of Family.. 291
Lori L. Dixon, Ed.S.

Extra-Ordinary Kingdom Ambassadors 307
Kim Vastine

Closing.. 319
Lori L. Dixon, Ed.S.

Meet the Authors 321

introduction

Lori L. Dixon, Ed.S.

Welcome to Wisdom on the Walk, where women's faith-inspired journeys of life are shared to ignite your own through revealing the truth of God, His Kingdom, and embracing circles of influence and impact.

> "The Lord gives the word (of power); the women who bear and publish (the news) are great hosts." Psalm 68:11 Amplified Classic.

> "And the Lord answered me and said, 'Write the vision and engrave it so plainly upon tablets that everyone who passes may (be able to) read (it easily and quickly) as he hastens by.'" Habakkuk 2:2 Amplified Classic.

I am a visionary, or some would say a "seer" for God, as well as an "epiphany" expert, seeing how the "ah-has" of your life can lead to transformation and healing. My companies, LLD Legacy Publishing and Walk with Lori, are the vehicles for mission and ministry to share with others, including YOU.

Bringing four decades of wisdom and experience into the work that God has led me to do now, He continues to move us forward. My newest endeavor is attaining my certification as Prophet and Pastor in the Legacy International Bible School with Pastor Jody Glass, my sister. You will hear more about our story together in one of my chapters. I can't wait to share it with you!

I am an author and publisher of children's books, anthologies, non-fiction, and a multiple international award-winning host and producer on streaming TV with the ZondraTV Network. While working on Bravo's Real Housewives of Dallas with some of my fabulous celebrity clients, I learned about the further "realities" of how the chapters of our lives may be rewritten at any time.

As a believer in finding the heartstrings in life, releasing the strongholds of fear, and living the life God designed for you, I was recently pushed hard by God to begin a new, enhanced journey that even I hadn't expected. I believe that we are all SEEN in our God-given creation and are responsible for sharing it in this world, at this time, and in the way God's Kingdom depends.

What IS this new expected journey that God so eloquently orchestrated?

How did this all begin?

I am excited to share this divinely-given story of how Wisdom on the Walk was born. In December 2022, God instructed me to begin writing my newest book. He shared the title with me as Wisdom on the Walk. God led me to some of the many stories and other writings He nudged me to collect since my last book, *Step OUT, Step UP, Step Forward: How to Walk in Your Purpose*, was published. Since then, God has revealed His plan and desire for my life and work to be solidly grounded in Biblical principles. He has literally placed barriers and removed people and things from my life where His work and presence were not the main focus. After I finished the last book, God demanded that I pay attention to the wisdom along my walk of faith. He led me every step of this journey while also providing me with gifts that help to impact the lives of others to glorify Him.

God repeatedly prompted me to practice what I had learned, where wisdom was found, and how to translate the learning to my clients and others. So I kept these treasures of triumphs and even tragedies, as well as highlights and hurdles for God to use for the assignment and mission He continues to have me walking.

While in prayer to ask for His guidance in the new project I thought I was working on, He said, "You will be writing this book with twelve women." What? Did I hear Him correctly? God continued to share how these twelve women would be the tribe to begin the ripple for women within their mission and outreach. Wow! What a shock, but how fabulous…of course, God created it! Why twelve? Didn't the disciples start with 12 as they learned, wrote, and walked OUT into the world with their commission and assignments? Each assignment was personalized for where they would go, what stories of Jesus and God would be told, and how they would begin the "rippling" process across the land. Did you know that it is said that within the early disciples of the twelve, they increased to 72 disciples? Many were women, as they ventured out where God sent them to spread the GOOD NEWS.

So, what did I say to God? I'm IN! I then asked God, "How will I find them?" He told me I would receive each of their names to invite personally. So, twelve it IS, and I cannot wait for YOU to meet them and hear their profound stories of love, loss, life, family, faith, and of course, how God played a role in each of their lives through their walks.

Here are the TWELVE:

- Shae Stewart
- Deanna Blair
- Jackie Davis
- Judy Cochrane
- Kim Vastine
- Stephanie Vasquez
- Lulite Ejigu
- Krista Medlock
- Irum Jones
- Molly Brown
- Becky Dozeman
- Allison Byrd-Haley

God also gave me the format AND, crazy enough, the marketing of it. I was genuinely astonished. He depicted how I would design an Academy for the authors and team to interact, learn, connect, write, and GROW. Am I still an author in this beautiful book? Yes! My stories will be interlaced with and between the other chapters to weave a tapestry of faith and hope.

The program Wisdom on the Walk... WoW, Academy, and it has been a WOW journey! We have become a community of spirit-filled authors, a group of women guiding and providing a legacy to support YOU!

We are blessed to have a fantastic team to walk WITH our women and to support me in this extraordinary process.

Meet them...

- Shae Stewart: author, editor, and collaborative partner
- Jordan Mitchell: virtual assistant and supportive editor
- Kim Gosnell: final editor, ghostwriter
- Callie Revell: graphic designer, book layout specialist, social media designer
- Jordan Gosnell: illustrator and graphic artist

It has become the Wisdom on the Walk as we each place our feet, sometimes walking forward, sometimes curling up in the comfort zone, and other times off the path until God's guidance shifts us back where He wants us walking for and always toward Him.

This book is not just another anthology of women's stories but a call for you... a collective of heartfelt connections to your life, spoken through another woman's moments with God, words for you to reflect and see your specific circumstance where God wants YOU to see Him with you. There are prayers to support you in reaching out and spending time with the Holy Spirit to nurture, listen, and guide you through the trials and the triumphs. God speaks directly to YOU; we are only conduits of His LOVE and relationship with Him. Will you receive the call?

Join us on the JOURNEY of
Wisdom on the Walk
Spirit-filled, God-directed,
purpose-driven LIFE stories

Sincerely YOURS,

lori l. dixon

Lori L. Dixon, Ed.S.

wisdom in the meantime

Krista Medlock

"Where shall I go from your Spirit? Or where shall I flee from your presence?" Psalm 139:7

A thirteen-year-old girl wrote a letter to herself in the refuge of her room titled "A Vow to Myself." It began with words, "I vow constant and everlasting strength to better myself...." Three notebook pages and numerous red markings later, it closed with the words, "I vow to try my hardest to stay firm, cherish and honor my vows to myself."

Little did she know that at 43 years old, she would discover that her calling and unique gifting were given life in

1,500 innocent and faith-filled words. That girl is me. The letter foretells a testimony of purpose and reassurance in my walk "in the meantime" to my God-given calling. I cannot wait to unveil God's promises and plan for me revealed in my letter before I knew Christ. I cannot wait to show the sweetness of "in the meantime" when I share what awaits as you come through it on the other side.

"In the meantime" is defined as "the time before something happens or before a specified period ends" and "while something else is being done or was being done." This means we are in constant motion, active and present. "In the meantime" gives us the gift of growth and progress through time. All the Lord requires of us is obedience and acknowledging His sovereignty in our walk. John 5:8 reads that Jesus said to him, "Get up, take up your bed, and walk." Therefore, our in the meantime" MEANS something.

I have had my share of "in the meantime" and continue to, which are often characterized by uncertainty, stagnancy, and confusion. Our life is a continuum of "in the meantime" that leads us to our ultimate purpose, legacy, and everlasting. It is a necessary facet of our walk. The Lord prunes us while assembling the next dimension of our faith. I genuinely believe that my letter to myself, rather God's letter from Him through me, is God's way of saying, "I can show you better than I can tell you."

When I look at my faith journey thus far, I always yearn for His presence "in the meantime." I would envy those that spoke of their experiences with Him. Growing up in the church, I heard others talk about the love of Christ with so much faith and conviction. Tears of joy rolled down their faces at the mention of His name. I listened to them intently as believers would share encounters and conversations with Him in His undeniable presence. Yet, I remember thinking, why do I not experience His presence? How is it that I am left living my life without His presence? So, my prayers have been, "Show me your presence and guide me, Lord." Sometimes, I am so desperate for His love and attention that I call out, "Jesus!"

There is a scripture that can only describe what happens next in my life. "Where shall I go from your Spirit? Or where shall I flee from your presence?" (Psalm 139:7). When you ask, He answers.

From that day forward, the Lord and I have shared God-sightings. God-sightings are what I refer to as timestamps of His presence. They are sweet and tender, "knowing" that He is right where you are. God-sightings, in the meantime, demonstrate His unique love for me and His very personal presence in my life. As we grow closer, He reveals himself "at the present moment" and offers recollection and revelation of times where He was ever-present in the past. My biggest elevations, significant breakthroughs, and sweetest blessings were disguised "in the meantime." Each God-sighting reaffirmed my calling and purpose while pointing my focus to Christ and His plan.

The day that I found the letter to myself was a God-sighting. He showed me who I had become through Him by reading the letter aloud after years of being buried in a storage box. Of course, your God-Sightings will be unique to you and your call, but I would like to encourage you with examples of some of my God-sightings that declare my identity and purpose through Christ.

Early Childhood: In the meantime, He draws us near…

At four years old, we moved to Dallas from Houston. My mom took us to a local church for a visit. I don't remember the context of the sermon, but I clearly remember when the pastor opened the opportunity to join the church. I felt called to "come" to the front. I didn't know what he asked the congregation, but I walked to the pulpit. And so it was; we (mom and family included) were church members. That is where I met my best friend Dana, who is still one of my best friends. That is where my journey in faith began. Later in my teens, I daydreamed of that moment that would assign significance to that day when I assuredly walked up to that pulpit...a god-sighting.

Excerpt from my letter: "I vow to keep the Lord in my heart and mind daily. This includes my activeness in the choir, UMYF (United Methodist Youth Fellowship), usher board, and any other leadership role in the church."

Teen Years: In the meantime... He plants seeds...

My childhood was somewhat sheltered as my dad was strict and restrictive. I spent most of my spare time alone in my room, left to daydream. This also shows the Lord's provision and grace in not-so-perfect circumstances. My capacity for revelation, future-focused thinking, and innovation expanded in those times of isolation. As I shared, at thirteen, I was so brokenhearted about my dad's strict rules I wrote a letter to myself, proclaiming who I wanted to become as an adult and what I wanted to accomplish. I still needed to learn what was being set in motion. Upon finding and rereading the letter, I could not believe what I had read. It was not happenstance. As you will see throughout this chapter, it was a God-sighting in its purest form.

Early 20s: In the meantime... He saves us...

College was a pivotal time when I deviated from my faith. I don't think I stepped foot in a church or even prayed for the first two years of my college journey. Not proud, but nothing is wasted. He used even that time to grow deeper in my relationship with Him. I joined a praise choir, but only for friendships and outings. Our choir was invited to sing at a conference in a city nearby. That weekend, we all jumped in cars and headed down the road in collegiate fashion. Music was blaring. Five different conversations were buzzing in the front and back seats. Amid all the happenings, I was in the back, middle seat, "on the hump," as we called it.

I knew that I didn't "belong" there at that moment. I was uneasy. All of a sudden, an unwieldy force overtook me and the car. Shouts and screams drowned out the music, and sounds of scraping and hard metal resounded, culminating in a violent crash. Do you know that expression, "Everything happened so fast"? Well, it did. Here is where it gets good. I could

"Your *in the meantime* MEANS something."

krista medlock

have quickly been ejected through the front windshield. The right conditions were at play for that to happen—and nothing was stopping me—no seatbelt, middle hump seat, and literally tons of blunt force. God saved me and the others in the car that day. No matter what choices we make, His mercy endures. He is looking after us in all situations. There is no force stronger than God. He spares our lives so that we can accomplish His plan for us.

Excerpt from my letter: "I vow to make wise and conscious decisions for myself and myself alone."

The late 20s: In the meantime, He prompts...

I was fortunate to climb quickly in my career. I became a Director of Marketing at a large global manufacturing facility and was exposed to influential connections and mentors. One of my business trips revealed a bigger purpose for me. I attended an industry conference called ISPA (International Spa Association), where a speaker, who was a former talk show host, Bertice Berry, gave a powerful talk. I remember very little of her speech. But I will never forget how energized I was. I remember feeling a fire in my belly!

Having so much admiration for her, I approached to meet her. Before I could gather my words, she said, "You are going to be on a mountaintop." I was speechless. God speaks through others to prepare your heart, incite vision, and prompt action… another God-sighting that would plant the seed for drive and ambition.

Excerpt from my letter: "I vow to make goals and to accomplish them… I vow to keep a high self-esteem… I will be confident everywhere and in anything I do."

The early 30s: In the meantime, He guides and reminds…

A few years later, I was at a women's conference where Priscilla Shirer was speaking. Remember that fire in my belly I told you about? It would show up again and overwhelm me. I was on a spiritual high. At the close of her keynote, one of the ladies sitting near me pulled me aside and said, "You will be up there speaking before women. You will own a business that supports women in business". I was not convinced, nor did I receive her message. I did not want to own that kind of business and was offended by what she said. Ha! Unbeknownst to me, God was working on my heart and my path. Several years later, I was standing at the registration table of a women's event, and joy flooded my spirit. At that moment, a memory invaded my thoughts, one of Stacie Ansell sharing with me that I would own a business for women in business.

But this time, I wasn't upset. I was grateful. I didn't tell you that I was standing at the registration desk of my event, one of many hosted by my own company, The Girl Cave... which supports women and women in business. It was our first anniversary. I did feel called to start The Girl Cave but had not connected it to what occurred that day several years back. That year was a faith journey to build and create community, so I began.

Excerpt from my letter: "I vow to meet new people... I vow to establish good sociability...."

The late 30s: In the meantime, He strengthens and comforts...

I experienced my first true heartbreak. I had never experienced hurt and betrayal quite like that. I was stuck in that anger and knew I needed to move forward. I could not let go and forgive. While I didn't pray, my heart was calling to Jesus. I didn't have the words and felt too weary. But He provided the words needed on my behalf. One day I was driving with no real destination, simply driving to distract my mind. I was in my thoughts, replaying all the offense of the heartache. Suddenly, the sun poured through my front window. It was so powerful that it disrupted my thoughts. It shone on my face, and I experienced an inexplicable peace and beauty. The words "His face shines upon you" spoke in my spirit. I drove home and immediately searched for those words in scripture, and there it was, "The Lord Bless you and keep you, the Lord make His face shine upon you and be gracious to you; the Lord turn His face toward you and give you peace." Numbers 6:24-26. The blessings in this scripture declare that God will "keep" you, be "gracious" to you and give you "peace." His words and our reflection of His word can reassure, protect, and support. They are full of grace, making all situations better than they were otherwise. Moments of God's grace in our lives and those around us strengthen and comfort us so we can forgive, love, and move forward, offering testimony where opportunity avails itself.

Excerpt from my letter: "I vow to be with my friends through hard times and offer good advice and support. I vow to be kind to everyone and establish healthy relationships."

Early 40s: In the meantime... He elevates us...

COVID proved to be a challenging and bleak few years. Many people, myself included, did not bear much fruit. But what it represented refined many souls. It was undoubtedly an "in the meantime" that did not have an end in sight. Consequently, I became hypersensitive to this precious life we must live.

While shackled by world events, I searched for what life meant to me. The routine of Sunday was in play. I went to church service, came home, and continued life as usual. However, one service reinvented life for me in a moment. I usually don't pay attention to the announcements during the service, and I wasn't paying attention this particular Sunday. Then, I heard one word, "Honduras," and I came to full attention. In the past, when I would listen to the word "mission," I drifted away, not paying attention. But this time was different. I felt prompted to "GO." Unfortunately, I was disobedient and did not act immediately. It was weeks later that I inquired about going, and no spots were available. Immediately, I felt deeply saddened and convicted. The next few weeks haunted me as I felt I was missing the opportunity of a lifetime.

In the meantime, what happened could only be at the hand of God. I happened to be sitting at lunch after service, and I overheard someone say, "She will be unable to go." I turned to the person sitting next to me, and I asked what she was referring to, and she repeated that one mission member would be unable to go to Honduras, and a space opened up. I wasn't going to miss the opportunity to act this time!

I immediately ran to the pastor and said I wanted to go if it was open. In the next few weeks leading up to the trip, certain events only reaffirmed my belonging to the mission. He opened the door to renew my passport in New Orleans, the closest passport office available for an appointment to expedite the process. He shifted work obligations to alternative dates. He connected me with members who graciously provided intel on proper preparedness. And it all unfolded beautifully as the trip was, although cliché sounding, the experience of a lifetime. Those eight days of selflessness and giving changed my life forever. I find complete joy in serving others, so my life is forever richly blessed.

Excerpt from my letter: "I vow to smile as much as possible… I will cry, pray and talk to someone I trust whenever I need to release anger or sadness. I vow to make the best of my life by having as much fun as possible and enjoying myself and my life."

Today, I wake up with the expectancy of my sweet God-sightings. I pray for the same expectancy for you. In your "in the meantime," one encounter with the Lord is even greater than our wildest dreams. One experience with Him can eliminate all hurt, worry or fear. One hint of His presence can give you a lifetime of hope and joy.

Your "in the meantime" MEANS something. God woos us in the meantime, softening our hearts to His grace and drawing us back to Him and His unique plan for each of us. "And behold, I am always with you, to the end of the age" (Matthew 28:20).

In these times, nothing is wasted and used for your ultimate good. The word affirms, "All things work together for the good of those who Love God and are called according to His purpose."

What should my testimony of God-sightings MEAN to you and your "in the meantime"? Every season has purpose, and you're "in the meantime." We have established that the Lord is rooted, present, and in control of every facet of our lives. So, what are we called to do? What is our part? What you do in the meantime is CRITICAL. My trinity of walking through the meantime is reestablishing identity and purpose, building your faith, and serving others.

Your walk "in the meantime" to reestablish purpose...

You are the ONLY you in this universe. God intended it that way. I become overwhelmed with love and excitement when I think of that for myself. Wow!! There is only one ME!! We are a walking source of power and authority. You have a particular, God-appointed purpose and beauty that cannot be taken away, voided, or canceled. That is your POWER!

Declare a passion, goal, or dream revealed to you at some point. Please write it down.

Reflect and describe an experience you would consider a miracle or demonstration of His presence.

Your walk "in the meantime" to perfect your faith...

Faithfulness is full of flavor and has so much dimension. The "in the meantime" allows us to refine our faith in many ways. That makes each new day a host of possibilities.

Write a letter to yourself proclaiming your faith in the future—what you will become and accomplish. Then, reread it periodically and watch those words become God's promises.

Your walk "in the meantime" to serve others through your giftings…

One thing I have learned is that when we experience feeling meaningless or when we think that the Lord is absent, it frequently means that we are not using our gifts the way He intended.

Take inventory of your gifts and develop a plan to use them to serve others.

Write them down. Reevaluate often to ensure that you remain in alignment with your giftings.

Prayer to God

Reflect on the scriptures below. Then, ask God to reveal His message in walking through your "in the meantime."

"All things work together for the good of those who Love God and who are Called According to His Purpose." (Romans 8:28)

"And behold, I am always with you, to the end of the age." (Matthew 28:20)

Ask Him for supernatural energy and alertness as He reveals Himself to you personally. Then, write a prayer praising Him in the way you expect to see and experience Him each day.

I am profoundly praying for you as you awaken to your "God-sightings" during the "in the meantime" moments. Whether they bring joy, laughter, heartache, or insight, God is fully present, walking with you in each of them.

Reflection

All things work together for good...

Romans 8:28

dream big

Lori L. Dixon, Ed.S.

"Too many of us are not living our dreams because we are living our fears. Life has no limitations; except the ones you make."
—Les Brown

Joseph was a dreamer of BIG dreams. He was berated for those dreams and sold because of them. He believed and walked the path given in front of him and became jailed before he realized the importance of these dreams. Yet, he kept dreaming, marketed himself to the King to be his dream interpreter, and became royalty. The great "riches to rags to riches again" story. AND… God showed up in it all!

David was a dreamer, was challenged to be a warrior, and fought giants on the way to walking in his dream. And God showed up.

Moses was a dreamer as he heard the call of his people. However, fear got in the way as he wrestled with his insecurities about best assisting them. And God showed up!

Jonah was NOT a dreamer, yet God needed him. He chased him until he saw the dream, too. Which would you rather be, a Joseph or a Jonah? God always shows up where dreams are present. He wants to walk with you every step of the way when you want a relationship with Him.

- Are you dreaming big enough for God to walk right in and enhance your wildest thoughts and feelings about that dream?
- Do you have the heart of a dreamer?
- Can you dream it in all its brilliance and give it back to the ultimate dream giver, God?

They say, "If you can dream it, you can create it." Can you? If this is true, why is dreaming big so difficult for us? If you believe in the words of Les Brown, it is FEAR.

Our dreams shift us to thoughts of hope and opportunity and tap into the creative side of the mind where anything can happen. Dreams are powerful when paired with vision and possibility; bringing our desires into a real space of creation; encouraging us to stretch forward, imagine broader, and be impacted by the interactions we have in our lives.

When I think of dreams, I see lots and lots of BUBBLES!

Opening the view even wider and adjusting the lens to see the dream in full color and intensity is just the beginning. Our eyes shift to witness their vivid images. I see our dreams as bubbles floating around us and being activated in our life by just one breath of positive intention to soar from our past or present into our future, flowing in a path of color and light, inspiring us to keep moving forward and not let go.

I was known in my previous career as a speaker as the "bubble lady." When I traveled across different states, many times by car, I would carry bubbles in my center console. Then, during traffic, delays, or accidents, I would sit and blow bubbles, usually out of my convertible or sunroof openings. You should have seen the other drivers' faces.

I used bubbles in my therapeutic classrooms since breathing for children and youth with anxiety or attentional challenges were incredibly calming. I also used bubble blowing with different blower wands and items with my speech and language children to strengthen oral motor muscles, like lips, cheeks, tongue, and jaw. All my workshops have bubbles on the table, too. You must admit you love bubbles, or you did once. Now, as a Nana, we always have bubbles available.

During one of these bubble-blowing sessions with adults, I saw the beautiful room filling with iridescent little globes of breath. The sunlight in our environment created this gorgeous view, and I realized these little spheres contained not only a breath but a thought, a moment, during our work together. It was a "press pause" moment for some people in the learning session. For others, it stimulated great thought, and for others, it unleashed calmness and a download minute of the intense connections they were making. For me, they became "dream bubbles." Recently, God reminded me to bring back the concept just for you.

Dreams can cause us to breathe deeply! Don't you always feel better when you are blowing bubbles? Sometimes overflowing laughter is even created. Bubbles help us breathe in a flow of sustained breath as we realign our prefrontal cortex to relax. With an "hahhhhh" breath or even humming, we vibrate and stimulate our Vagus nerve to calm our bodies, releasing adrenaline trapped and replacing it with dopamine and oxytocin. You may have heard how dopamine is the happy hormone, and oxytocin is the cuddle hormone. Can you imagine how amazing we can feel as we dream big, breathe deeply, and create a "haaaahhhhh" breath response that floods our bodies with positive feelings?

These "Dream bubbles" of breath-focused thoughts on one memory or insight can appear as more than a basic feeling or episodic memory. It can be one moment you want to remember that applies to your dream moving forward through a past and even present-focused image or vision. It can be a dream you could never let go of without a way to release it or connect it to what "may" be. Some dream bubbles are a moment in time we want to experience over and over and over again when we need it most. Those moments which take our breath away or make us sigh deeply fuel us to walk forward on our dream "path" in a big way.

When he was little, my grandson, Clark, struggled with changes and transitions. So we designed a way for him to embrace what may be coming in the moments ahead for him, to be present in THIS small way and breathe IN all its goodness, releasing all the fear or anxious thoughts. We had him visualize a small bubble he controlled… putting his little fingers around and blowing gently as the bubble grew and grew in front of him, just like blowing a real bubble. Yet, this bubble never popped unless HE decided it would pop, leaving us laughing even more. Sometimes he would let the bubble go and watch it float away in the house, out the window, or up in the air, just like his fear or apprehension around something. Plus, it created the breath needed to relax his brain and let him know there was no threat, and the laughter enhanced serotonin and dopamine, too.

We still love to use this with both grandchildren today. They love blowing bubbles outside, catching them, popping them, and having control over the bubble gives them feelings of release and support. Clark and Logan both pretend to blow bubbles when we are calming down or settling in for a story as they sleep. Those bubbles give them relaxation and a way to let the challenges of the day float by wherever we want to place them. We also stick our best dreams into those bubbles to see them later. Bubbles are powerful imagery for us in life.

> "Divine promotion (of God's dreams in your life) is better than self-promotion."
> —John Maxwell

John C. Maxwell is a significant proponent of the dreams within us. I love his book, *Put Your Dream to the Test*, and I have used it myself and with clients for many years. He talks about dreaming your dreams big enough so GOD can step in and make them happen, not only big enough for you. God brings forth the miracles he has instilled and planted within us to be dormant until precisely the right time he needs us. Then, He walks those dreams with us every step of the way.

"God brings forth the miracles he has instilled and planted within us to be dormant until precisely the right time he needs us."

lori l dixon

One of my dreams over the last year was to write my next book to glorify my relationship with Christ and my Father God. As I have shared in another chapter, that dream I thought was coming to fruition was enhanced by the additional inclusion of twelve other powerhouse women for you to hear how God has been present in their lives. So we are all walking together in the community to bring this new model of book, crafted by our Father, to share the stories, dreams, visions, and transformations being realized and traveled again right now...FOR YOU! God is good! My original dream sure got a LOT BIGGER in HIM!

If you have not read *The Dream Giver* by Bruce Wilkinson, it is a wonderful place to understand and embrace the dream "bubbles" from God, created for you to meet a GREAT NEED in His world right now. He shares a fantastic quote: "The BIG DREAM is what God has laid a hold of you to do. And, unfortunately, it is never too late to act on your dream. Just ask Moses." YOU are in great company!

We can glean much from the story of Moses. Bruce Wilkinson shares the following points for us to know:

1. A big dream is always overwhelming at first.
2. Josie Bisset says, "Dreams come in a size too big so that we can grow into them."
3. Ultimately, a big dream aims to meet a BIG NEED in the world.
4. While you still have breath, it's never too late to act on your dream. (There's the bubble and breath relationship. Keep blowing and release the struggles!)

God supports and even speaks to us in our dreams, whether prophetically or as quiet, gentle remembrances of Him in our life. I journal mine when I wake up from a rather impactful one and during the day from the prophetic words and visuals God gives me for others and myself. He is alive within us, giving us the nudge to walk into more steps in our purpose and assignment for his Kingdom expansion. How could we not DREAM BIG when we are builders for a supernatural and spiritual Kingdom on Earth? God is constantly stretching us and guiding us to stay on the path He has laid before us. Can't you feel it?

Why does dreaming BIG scare us? As one of my clients has shared with me. Elizabeth was aware of all the passions in her life and was walking boldly in some of the areas where she was called to engage her talents and gifts. Her mission was beautiful, yet the scope of the dream was still only what she could see, feel, hear, and touch. Could she dream bigger? That was the task we tackled together. Stretching so far and seeing those dream bubbles around us as they drift upward or in front of us effortlessly is just a step in the process. Elizabeth and I would dream so big it freaked her out. Then we let the greatness of God carry us further in purpose. Her daily intentions were set, and manifesting was happening. I could see just enough before her to know it was a breathtaking view. She began to float and walk in her new dreams, brilliantly embracing them with excitement and anticipation. Dream big enough for God to rush inside and perform miracles leads us to elevate our grounded thoughts and leap with purpose.

Ask yourself, will I walk, fly, or leap into what's next? Sometimes we walk, fly, and sometimes... we leap... and blow a few bubbles as you DREAM BIG!

Prayer to God

Father, I know you see the big dream in me before I even see it. Let it come forth in the timing designed by you in the manner necessary to bring forth glory and honor to you…in other words, your beautiful and perfect timing. May it leave a legacy on earth and in heaven as the Kingdom you are building requires. May I understand the dream enough to let it become a passion and mission on earth. I don't always dream BIG enough for your wisdom and ideas to enter. So let me be fearless and focused on YOUR will and needs as each breath brings the dream inside me, designed by YOU! Amen!

Reflection

there is a time for everything and a season for every activity under the heavens

Ecclesiastes 3:1

rooted and established in christ

Jackie Davis

"Do not forsake wisdom, and she will protect you; love her, and she will watch over you. Wisdom is supreme; therefore, get wisdom. Though it costs all you have, get understanding. Esteem her, and she will exalt you; embrace her, and she will honor you." Proverbs 4:8-10 NIV

Every year, I pray for a word or phrase I may use as a compass or measure for character or spiritual growth. In 2022 my word was "wisdom." I prayed to God for wisdom, not from raising my IQ or becoming a scholar but from God's divine essence. My very Spirit was craving a deepening of wisdom that would open my heart to steadfast faith, direct my steps to where He wants me to walk, and be deeply rooted within His word to grow vital significance in my life's calling, purpose, and fulfillment. I prayed for Him to plant me like a tree by the river so I could taste the living waters and not wither away in a fruitless life. I yearned to experience a conscious understanding of the Fruit of His Spirit and give birth to these fruits deep within me with a deeper embrace and conviction. I desired to become a better servant, live beyond myself for others, and better understand His grace, compassion, and mercies. I knew this year would be a year of complete spirit, mind, and soul surrender while becoming the clay within the potter's hand, submerged into the fire for ultimate refinement, molding, and reshaping, in which I would endure the chipping away at the fabric of myself to become transformed in my core by His wisdom, and by His very hands. How dare I ask for such wisdom, or better yet, was I truly prepared for the lesson to sit, listen, and be transformed? Yet, I had a sense of the magnitude that would come from choosing this word.

> "If you wait at wisdom's doorway, longing to hear a word for every day, joy will break forth within you as you listen for what I'll say." Proverbs 8:34 TPT

As my journey began in 2022, I was already at the midpoint of embarking on an uprooting journey with my husband, in which we moved from Texas to Oklahoma and bought some land to build a forever home. We signed our contract in March 2021, expecting to move into our new home in December. For the record, my word for 2021 was "joy." To say I had to cling to joy that year is an understatement. I quickly learned that joy is not the same as happiness.

Joy is rooted within God, part of His character, a Fruit of the Spirit. It is what will keep us grounded in hope amid a storm only because we've experienced His unfailing love. God is not a God that would lie and contradict himself or ask you to step out of a boat in faith as He did with Peter in the middle of the ocean, just to let you sink and drown. He will always make a way with His faithfulness and provision. God does not only see us; He wants us to experience the joy of life. But that's another story for later.

Moving to Oklahoma was a big decision for my husband and me; we felt pulled to move closer to one of our daughters and her family. We sold our home in Texas several years earlier and made decisions that would change our lives and those we love that we left behind. Did I mention that although my husband can work remotely from home, he periodically must travel to his headquarters office in Texas? This made us feel secure knowing our loved ones and the relationships we were leaving behind would remain close due to our regular visits. More than anything, we felt a great peace from God leading us to this new chapter in our lives and shared much joy and anticipation in building this new house.

I was also looking forward to the new friendships and sisterhood possibilities for expanding my women's mission (Pinky Swear Mission) or possibly beginning a new women's group, finding a new church, leading and participating in bible studies and women's gatherings, and helping build community. There was no reason for this to be challenging since I love serving and supporting people, seeing women walking in their purpose, being empowered, and succeeding. So yes, I dove right in and soon started meeting women in my new community. I even received an invitation to join one of the women's neighborhood committees, which I accepted with much delight and eagerness.

Initially, I felt welcomed. However, growing and building new friendships in that group was short-lived. Yes, you read correctly; very short-lived. I soon learned they criticized me for my beliefs and told me that despite being women of faith, to "stop preaching" and that I was overzealous in serving others. One woman remarked, "That's not how things work here." This group of women went as far as to reach out to my daughter behind my back to have her ask me to step down from their committee before they ultimately removed me from it themselves.

Do you remember me saying earlier that my word for 2021 was "joy," so you can see how clinging to joy during this time was challenging? I cannot begin to make up this true story! However, in all fairness to this group of women, I will not share the whole story because they are not here to tell their side, much less defend themselves. After prayers and conversations with God, I've laid this entire situation at His feet, taken ownership of my role, and hold no ill feelings toward anyone. However, I need to share a short snippet of this story to communicate better how God was preparing to stretch me, bring me into a sweet surrender of leaning into Him, and grace me with His wisdom. Remember me praying for God's "wisdom" this year, 2022? I wondered what I was walking into, feeling disillusioned toward authentic friendships, much less building sisterhood relationships, and even doubting serving the community where my hubby and I were building our forever home. I also missed my precious relationships from Texas and the gatherings of women with like-minded spirits. I second-guessed many things, especially relationships outside my husband and the Lord. Yet, I knew how to serve my community, make friends, empower women, and grow authentic friendships. So, why this proverbial desert? Little did I realize the lesson He was preparing for me. It was on me to pause to hear what the Lord was saying. As Katrina Mayer says, **"Wisdom doesn't come from speaking. It comes from listening."**

I thought I knew whom I was bringing to Oklahoma when I thought about myself, and I was not arrogant in thinking, **"Rooted and grounded in Christ's love is the path of abundant life!"** As women, or as his daughters, we still experience life's trials and tribulations. We, as his daughters, are not removed from the struggles just because we walk as believers; we come out of the battles differently. But, as we emerge victorious with confidence from the spiritual battlefield, the wounds we have survived become like a shiny medal placed upon our armor. The same armor provided to us by Him, our heavenly father. Or, in some cases, we walk away with a beautiful, rare gem upon our crown, representing our healing of what we endured or the lessons we learned while in the trials we overcame. The Lord's grace for us during difficult times is not like a bragging rights trophy. On the contrary, it teaches us humility. It's His love covering us so that we may endure, overcome and come out with stronger resilience in character so that His light will shine within us and His love is seen through us.

Understanding my identity in Christ as a woman in this life walk has been the grandest, most humbling experience I have ever encountered. Soon, I felt His embrace deep in my soul, tugging at my very Spirit that He breathed life into when He created me and placed me in my mother's womb. I felt His wisdom pour into me, refining me with His scriptures, worship songs, praises, my writings, quiet times, and reminiscing of things gone by. I missed a step or two in life or relationships with other people. He took me to places where I gained valuable lessons and found genuine, authentic relationships. Yet, His grace was sufficient to remind me that His love saved and redeemed me. He brought me here to remind me that it is in Him that I am rooted and established, not in the world. I needed to lean in and listen because His work and purpose within me were far from done, and He required me to refocus. He called me to a city I did not know, an unknown land to build a new home, where I only knew my daughter and her family. However, in the grand scheme of His plan for the construction of a new home, He also planned to isolate me, refresh me, and rekindle my Spirit. He drew me closer to Him to remind me of His love so that I could come to renew and finish the work He created me to do. My entire being came to a crossroads with Him regarding why this was happening. I had gotten in my way, and things blurred my vision and understanding of the work ahead of me. These lessons were divinely appointed to me by God to grow me in ways that I could not do alone. I knew He was trying to get my undivided attention.

"We are the vessels of life, and with such power comes great responsibility to nurture life, harness love, and build communities."

jackie davis

After all, this year, I prayed for His wisdom. It meant I had to stop what I, "Jackie," was doing and be still and reach my full potential in him. I also needed to remember the past lessons that would catapult me to a new start, a refreshing approach to what He had already taught me and created within me to fulfill His purpose and calling in my life. The life that I breathe and walk for Him, in His love, and to empower other women to understand His creation and purpose in us as women.

When you hear and experience Him, you know a certain peace. Soon the unfolding before me, the stillness, and the lessons all began to manifest. Aww, I love the sweet sound of His voice. It's like honey and milk, my dear sister. **His sheep hear His voice, recognize it, and follow Him.** Realization began amid the words and phrases I had prayed for throughout the years that would become a compass or measure for my character or spiritual growth. I started with a few of them, joy in 2021, wisdom in 2022, and walking in clarity and intention in 2023. Then finally, I knew where to get refreshed and where to drink from the living waters, realizing there are places where my cup is filled with abundant blessings. There are other places where others emptied my cup. However, my cup has never broken, maybe dirtied or tarnished, but my cup in Him has never broken, and my place at the table was never taken away from me, or at least not by Him.

My sister, do you have an annual word or phrase that you pray to Him for? How long has your word for the year been so instrumental to you? Or have your yearly words and those timely lessons, regardless of their valuable contribution, faded away with every passing year? The focus on my annual word choices is memorable because I fully embrace them and seek Him to guide me where He needs me. **I want that for you too, my sister.**

I want to take you back to the completion of the building of our forever home. The process took longer than anticipated, fifteen months to be exact. My husband and I visited our property daily. We dedicated our new home to Christ with prayers and scriptures inscribed within the framing process. And we even had a bible placed within the center walls of our home. It became the haven, a peaceful dwelling for our marriage, and the house built by our Lord's love for us. During this time, he showed me that those yearly words and phrases I had earnestly prayed for Him to show me were substantial building blocks for the continual growth of my character and Spirit, just like His word is my daily bread and living water to my soul. I realized that He was speaking to me beautifully and enormously! His wisdom revealed itself during this time, leading me to a significant realization. I was not living up to my fullest potential for Him! I was allowing the enemy to rob me of my identity in Him, including my calling and voice. I needed to use every lesson, every word He had already spoken, and life over me to write and fill the pages of books used to influence women's lives through his revelations to me of his teachings and to share my testimony to empower women. All to help advance His kingdom through His wisdom and love.

> "...So that Christ may dwell in your hearts through faith. And I pray that you, being rooted and established in love, may have power, together with all the Lord's holy people, to grasp how wide and long and high and deep is the love of Christ and to know this love that surpasses knowledge—that you may be filled to the measure of all the fullness of God." Ephesians 3:17-19 NIV

The value of my everyday lessons continues to show a transformational effect on my spiritual growth, the knowledge of my mind, and the feeding of my soul. My place in Him has not yet reached a full circle of completion, and I have yet to use all the gifts and talents He has poured into me. I went dormant in my calling as a Spiritual Life Coach. However, he has shown me grace on the way back to them by reminding me of the mission and the path for His purpose for me, which is to share His love for us, his daughters, to shed some light on His creation of a woman, which was by no means an accident or a mistake because He makes no mistakes! I am deeply drawn to inspire women to discover deeper spiritual intimacy with Him and to reach their potential in Christ. **We are the vessels of life, and with such power comes great responsibility to nurture life, harness love, and build communities.**

My understanding of Him is different from that of a theologian or great scholar, and I understand Him by taking His yoke upon me and learning from Him. I dig deep into His words as often and intently as possible. Therefore, I can share how remarkable the gentleness of His power is when He designs a path for you that only you can fulfill.

Through the uprooting from Texas to Oklahoma, the realization that it was to serve as a reminder that God has shown me His grace, promises, the power of His Spirit, the covering of His armor, the sweetness of His fruit, but most of all, He has given me His unfailing love. He reminds me that the most important and significant relationship is with Him. And rejection from others isn't a personal attack. It ended up being a gift. I am fully aware, and He nudges me when I forget that my calling is to empower women in their purpose so that together as His daughters, we may be the change in a world that has gone cold toward His creation in humanity. I am committed and compelled to dig deeper into my relationship with Christ. I yearn to share with those with a similar fire in their Spirit to share and transform in Christ's wisdom. **We are the women of a new calling.** Yet, how many are willing to rise to the responsibility we are called to be as vessels of life?

I invite you to join me on this journey and to experience how deeply you, my sister, are rooted and established in our Lord's love. **He already chooses and celebrates you!**

Prayer to God

Dear Lord, let my life be a celebration of your creation in me. Allow me to be a light to someone else. Allow my thoughts to seek you, my heart to yearn for your ways, and may only you direct my steps. Let me be something every minute of every hour of my life that serves you wholeheartedly. Let the Fruit of your Spirit be part of my teaching, character, and harvest. Let your armor be my shield and covering. Let me be sincere and courageous. Make me honorable in your eyes. Let me always remember what you, my Lord, have done for me. Push me to be faithful in advancing your kingdom, but more than anything, Lord, grant me your servant daughter to love as you do. AMEN.

Reflection

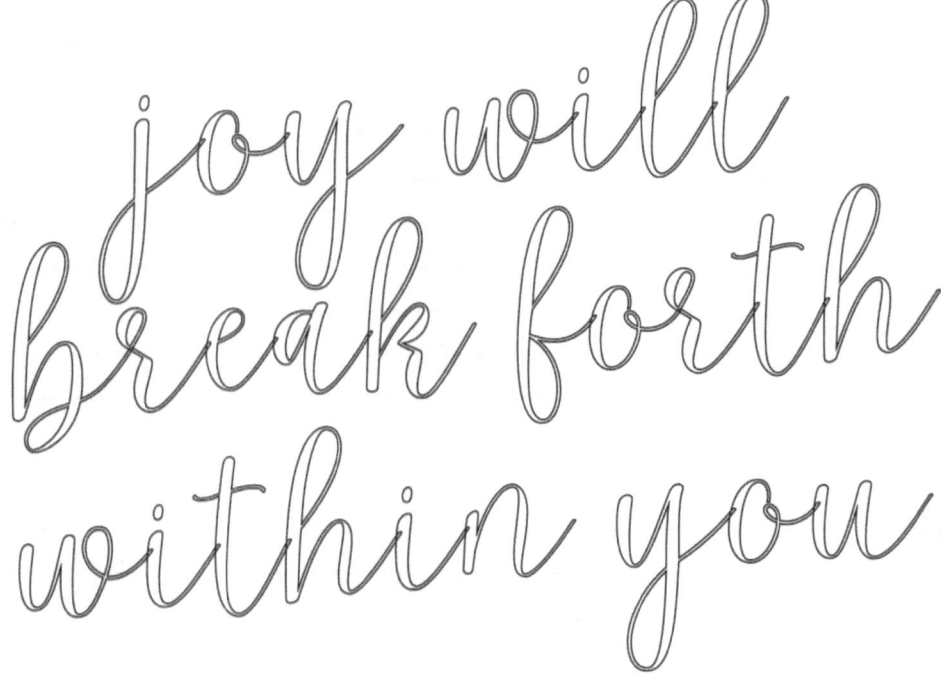

Proverbs 8:34 TPT

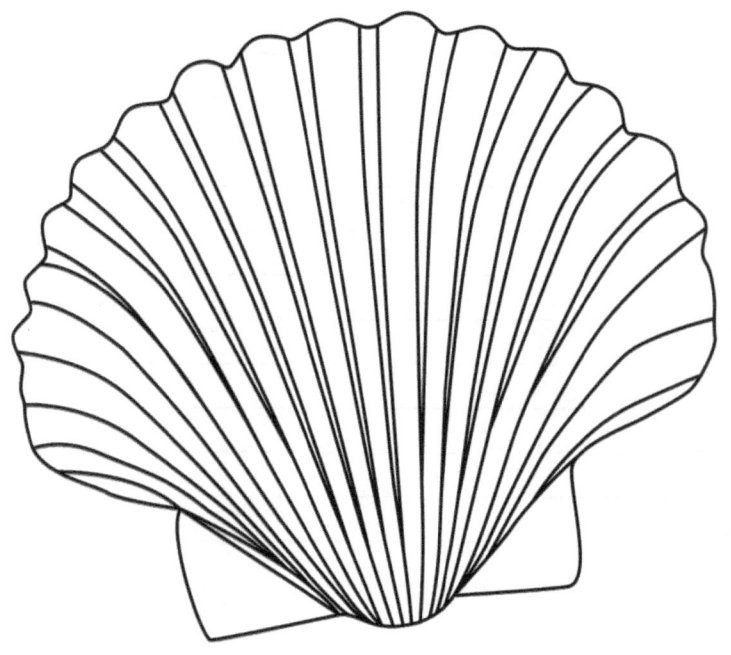

compassionate compass of life

Lori L. Dixon, Ed.S.

Years ago I was asked to speak for a special parents group, Compassionate Friends. I am honored to know about this unique and special organization. In my career and therapeutic work with children and families, I have referred families and individuals to the comfort of a chapter close to them so they may be embraced during their difficult times in loss and grief.

Since working with this group, I have been able to be present for numerous families as they are navigating the path of life along side of the grief of a child. Early in my career as I was working with families of children with chronic illness, life-threatening diseases, difficult health journeys, and the effects of these things on the dynamics of life. Have I experienced loss of my young, precious children clients, yet, and been blessed to sit with families at the time. It is a most difficult test of our faith in those moments, being able to listen and be still while offering compassionate words of support and memories when needed.

Do we need to work "with" the loss and grief of our life or "ride the waves" of the weeping, whether it may be a child or family member, or the great loss of a home, our health, or even a divorce? They are all losses and may be grieved during our walk of life. The scripture I have held on to much of my own life is Psalm 30:5. It has been there with me through love break-ups, death of a loved one, the loss of a friendship, or a way of life, an abandonment, and so much more. May its words speak to you now as you read them.

> "Tears may flow through the night, yet, joy (understanding, bliss, God's voice, the Holy Spirit's nudging, the ease, and sometimes the answers) comes in morning." Psalm 30:5

Weeping may remain for a night, but rejoicing comes in the morning.

The feelings we feel, regardless of why we feel them, may be characterized as pain found deep within us, within our soul. Loss can create a FEAR of never moving forward gain, never feeling whole, never feeling happy... stable... rested... or even ME. It can make us believe we will never enjoy life again, yet, God shines through amidst all of it. There is a moment of joy, newness, release, relief from the fear that had gripped us and making us immobile. God promises us life in Him through all of it, the obstacles, the delusion of even the word...NEVER. The only never we have within our life is that God will NEVER leave us or forsake us. The world may change, the circumstances or the familiarity of life may, but

God is a constant himself within us. His love never ends and never gives up on us, even when we are weeping, flowing fear in the darkest night of the soul, HE is always loving and compassionate for us.

Through it all, God is there. I want to share an illustration to give you a "life support" tool to be used when you most need it, not unlike these families or even as you go through these feelings of loss. As I struggled to understand the loss and tragedy of living without their child, I did walk with them in it and other great losses. This will have to be another story I share for you, as God is consistently wanting me to give you glimpses of my life, as He asks me to do with my own clients.

My husband and I love to travel and in his previous career he traveled for a living. I've been traveling since I was very young and always had an innate sense of direction. Yet in my life I needed guidance from wonderful parents and caregivers to understand where I was going. Years ago I wrote a poem about the Road of Life during some very turbulent and tragic times when even with my internal guidance system that my family and others had instilled in me, they couldn't help me in all choices and circumstances. Some of the words still ring within my ears… "the road of life is a hard road to travel, the road of life is a hard road to leave…" Yes, I felt that way during my life, no matter how my family loved me, I knew God was bringing me to so much more. I felt called at a young age to be there for others in their "road of life" experiences. I now, and probably always strived to support others in developing their life IGS through some of their most challenging paths and steps.

I want to honor each of you reading this book, in the journey you have been on in which the COMPASS of life and that IGS which guides you. It is there for us when we struggle, we fall, we release, and when we acknowledge our path, God steps in. He guides our steps because he wants us to walk more with him, in his name and to reach his mission for us in this life. YOU have been called for him and to embrace what destiny and authority is on our life. Yes, YOU… have this special assignment for your time on earth.

Understanding these "walks of life" require compassion for ourselves and others in their own paths. Yes? Compassion is giving love and care without expecting anything in return; listening and accepting where others may be in that moment and then in the next moment. Sometimes we feel there is no roadmap in life and what we believed was the journey is drastically halted and we become lost. I even call it "off roading". Can't you see it? Seeing others on the road, watching them struggle or even "own" their path, gives us the compassion to walk forward again.

The compass in life does not mean to "compare my journey to yours". My compass is designed especially for me, yet some concepts are similar. Hope is also an important part of the journey. Hope is the ability to transform my moment from "now" to "HOW" instead. "How" relies on the wisdom in GOD's directions. Have you ever stood still and felt like you were turning in a circle? Do you feel too many options from left to right to behind you and in front? Turning to God in these times, leaning in, embracing His will for you, and hearing his voice will continue to lead you and guide you gently and obviously with deep compassion for you, as his child.

These turns can be seen as the opportunities of N, S, E, and W. Not your typical north, south, east, and west, though. Just a way to remind you of how to make these turns and shifts in your life as you navigate the journey God is putting in front of you. He will always be there with you and for you. David, King David himself, felt lost many times throughout his process as a shepherd boy to King of great promise and chosen by God to lost without God. In Psalms he sings out to the Lord. As we walk through the darkest nights and valleys, God IS with us. This Psalm has been used in many meditations around loss and grief. I would like you to hear it a little differently.

> Yahweh is my best friend and my shepherd. I always have more than enough. (He gives me my needs and provides for me at all times.)
>
> He offers a resting place for me in his luxurious love.(for rest and refreshing time with Him)
>
> His tracks take me to an oasis of peace near the quiet brook of bliss. That is where he restores and revives my life. (He provides beauty around me in the nature he has provided and brings peace through this refreshment.)
>
> He opens before me the right path and leads me along in his footsteps of righteousness so that I can bring honor to his name. (He guides and is my internal guidance system as I align with him for the purpose he has placed within me.)
>
> Even when your path takes me through the valley of deepest darkness, fear will never conquer me, for you already have! (He is with us during the hills and the valleys of life, leading us through as a navigator. He will not let fear take over because we are walking with Him.)
>
> Your authority is my strength and my peace, the comfort of you love takes away my fear. (He wants what is best for us during times of loss, grief, uncertainty, and spiritual attack. He gives us strength through him, peace that is more than we can understand, and his undying love for us as his children.)
>
> I'll never be lonely, for you are near. You become my delicious feast even when my enemies dare to fight. (He prepares the table to receive us as his favorite guest during this time and protects us within his doors. No enemy will fight with us or attack when we are with him.)

You anoint me with the fragrance of your Holy Spirit, you give me all I can drink of you until my cup overflows. (He promises us the baptism through the Holy Spirit to be part of His divine family and places that IGS within us to use at all times. Overflowing our "cup" of goodness and mercy so not only we can drink to overflowing but we can share it with others around us who need to feel his presence.)

So, why would I fear the future? Only goodness and tender love pursue me all the days of my life. Then afterward, when my life is through, I will return to your glorious presence to be forever with you. (God's ultimate promise! Walking with him until it is time to go home. Every step in him is guided, guarded, and cared for through his grace and love. Wow…the "internal guidance AND protection system" is forever and when life is finished on this earth, it knows how to lead us how to him.).

Psalm 23 (The Passion Translation)

What a promise it is to live in his arms with him as the navigator of life! Here are a few ways to remember God's directions in life.

N: Nurture yourself in Him, pause, breathe in the bliss, and listen for God's quiet voice to walk further. Compassionate care should be practiced whenever you feel the connecting to the wisdom and principles of God are needed. Hope lies in this direction as we can experience the nurturing of ourselves and others. Hope is the view of our steps and our life forward. Hope is the snapshot of what is to

"What a promise it is to live in his arms with him as the navigator of life!"

lori l. dixon

come so we can remain in faith as we walk in newness to the next step in the journey.

S: Surround yourself with supportive and trusted others; stay connected; my grief is my grief...it will vary from family member to family member; hope lies in this direction as you rest of the arms of those who know the Lord, walk in his wisdom and truth and may have even walked a similar path of their own.

E: Express God's love, words, and compassion for other to receive along the road. Expressions of realness and truth are in the overflow God is providing you. This abundance can be shared with many in love and through words of continued hope.

W: Walk with confidence in knowing WHO you are in Christ, WHO is providing your IGS which is the Holy Spirit, WHERE you are walking for the Lord, and let no fear stop you along the way or create obstacles that you and God can't navigate through together. Share the wisdom of your walk with others and share God's words of care and kindness who have been ON the journey with you. You know our hope lies there.

One day I was speaking with my pastor at a relaxing pool party we were having for the youth in our church. He sat down next to me and asked me, "Do you grieve?" What an interesting question he posed and especially at a party with screaming and laughter as the tone of the day. I reflected for a moment before I responded to look inward and ask myself the same question. My inner talk went like this: "Why would I grieve? No one in my life had passed yet and I did have some relationship with grief in my daily work, yet, what a probing question. Wow...is this a time to witness to him and for me to have God speak through me to my own minister?"

I wrestled with my answer and finally, between what seemed like an eternity, I asked him, "why do you believe I grieve in my life?"

He smiled and proceeded to share with me that for sometime, knowing the work I do with families, children, and youth, he had been wanting to ask me how I deal with the overwhelming experiences they may be facing. I replied back that I am a "compassionate guide and friend" as they experience difficulties, loss, health challenges, and what we term as "chronic grief" in the therapeutic field. Thinking of some of the families that had gone through the deep loss of a child and how being there gave them a shoulder to lean on, a person to cry with or even release their anger as they struggled with the ending of a life they had been the caregiver and compassion-bringer for every day that child was on this earth. Eventually, I shared story after story of these families and the blessing of these children in their lives and in mine. How we are all forever changed by that ONE life God chose to come to earth for a purpose greater than we could ever imagine. How they children give more than they take from us and how their laughter, struggles, tenacious spirits, and joy-filled LOVE they give shows the face of GOD every day.

He smiled and nodded as I was defending my children and families who God had entrusted me and my purpose to at the time they needed it most. For a minute, he was speechless and kept his eyes fixated downward. He then raised his head up and looked at me directly in the eyes and in a firm, father-like tone, said, "they are you and with exactly whom God designed it to be for them on their journey, AND for you on yours. This won't be the only wisdom you gather either, Lori, but that will be up to you and our Father in Heaven to discuss next steps."

Wow! I felt it! I heard it! I knew it! It WAS the compass! God was steering the path we were on and the directions he gave were to strengthen my way and build my relationship with his tender most creation, his children. I saw God in that moment and was ready to continue walking forward in HIS knowing and purpose for me.

God's Compass can direct our path even when we feel lost in the moment and don't know where we are heading. As we know, no one provides us a complete "how to" map to walk our steps on our own. God provides all that we need exactly when we need it, whether it is a pause, a turn, a bridge, or sometimes a dead-end. He supports us as we find one that fits us and gives us continuous guidance. It is hope which sustains our belief while we keep the stories alive on the journey to share with others and to remember the unbelievable and supernatural experiences that happen.

Are you ready?

Prayer to God

Dear Lord, I thank you for these deep memories that remind us of your inner navigation and guidance system you have placed there to keep us on the walk of wisdom in our lives for YOU. Thank you for the compass you place within us to find YOU and walk with you. I thank you for always being there whether we are hurting or healing, listening or looking, or even resting and renewing…you continue to BE on the journey. You direct us in each turn and even "off roading" moments to navigate us back to your grace and compassion. May we be a conduit and supporter for each person you place within our lives to overflow our own cups you constantly give us in compassion and love. Amen.

If you are experiencing the loss of a child, please reach out to the Compassionate Friends network to find a chapter to support you on this journey to healing.

If you are in need of a support group for grief, reach out to a local church for the program many sponsor called, "GriefShare" to find a community to be part of your navigational team.

Be blessed in your journey!

Reflection

joy comes in the morning

Psalm 30:5

kingdom seeker

Shae Stewart

23 years old… I sat at the kitchen table of my parent's home, where I grew up from age five until I moved out at 18. I was hurting and seeking consolation from my mom, who was not a natural nurturer. Desperate because I was in excruciating emotional pain. I was lost. Yet another close friend had died unexpectedly. To make a horrible situation worse, it happened at our church camp. She was only 24 years old and had an aortic aneurysm. What?! Incomprehensible. I was devastated.

My mom an introvert but the most spirit-filled person I know. She loves Jesus with reckless abandon regarding her walk with Him. She was a first-grade teacher at our church's private school for thirty years. As she grabbed each piece of clothing from the dryer and folded them, she chose each word cautiously, as if she realized the importance of the message God passed through her mouth to my ears.

In her teacher's voice, she said, "Get a piece of paper and pen and write down the names of every person you've lost, how you knew them, and how they died." Wow! What did I do? I wrote. When I finished, tears flowing freely, I looked up and said, "There are more names on this list than the number of candles on my next birthday cake." She walked over and held me tight, telling me that God was still good, even though this hurt so much. "Oh, honey. I know this is so hard. Please remember His plan is perfect, whether we understand it or not. Life can hurt so much. He is still good and can be your best friend through this pain." I took in every word like a thirsty sponge in need of quenching.

I pondered if I am made in His image, and He is perfect, then I want Him to show me how to magnify and glorify Him, despite and through all of this pain.

How could He turn all the pain into a good thing? I was determined to find out. I was born in Dallas, Texas, in 1966 to a God-fearing couple. From an infant, in our home and our hearts, there was never a doubt about whether God existed or whether there was a Trinity. This was their firm foundation, which "rubbed off" my parents and into my soul. As many people do, I don't remember the date I gave my life to the Lord, but I know exactly where I was and how overwhelmed I felt by the Holy Spirit that evening. I knew without a doubt that I was a daughter of THE one true and living God who sent His son to take on every sin of every human from alpha to omega for ME… And for you.

In Junior high school, I had the incredible opportunity to take an elective class based on Zig Ziglar's book, *See You at the Top*, called "I Can." As an editor, I use words like "incredible" sparingly, but that class changed me and the trajectory of my life. I got a "check-up from the neck up," learned the meaning of a positive attitude, how to "eliminate stinking thinking," and avoid "hardening of the attitudes." Both of my parents are amazing people. But despite being married for 57 years before my D.O.D. (Dear Ol' Dad) died in 2020, they were never mistaken for Ward and June Cleaver, more like Archie and Edith Bunker. There were many generations of the passive-aggressive, negative-by-nature mentality. The lessons in that I Can class taught me how to think differently, respond lovingly, curb the reactive ridicule, and self-correct those tiny voices that tried telling me, "You can't." That class, orchestrated by God Himself, taught me to bring insightful knowledge into our home. My junior high elective class helped everyone in our household to profoundly improve our "glass-half-full" attitudes, even though I knew that was only the first step.

Fast forward from Junior High to the fun and carefree part of life, the late teens to early twenties. The decade where most young adults are partying, dating, spending their parents' money, studying, pledging, anticipating their futures, praying to get to the next phase, and enjoying every moment of being free. I struggled through those years. Don't get me wrong. I had a lot of fun, certainly more than my fair share during that era.

But I felt torn, as if I experienced guilt for being joyful, even after so much death in my world. Or on the other hand, I felt like I wasn't living my life's purpose when I had sad times that took me into depression and emptied my half-full-glass. I knew that God did not cause any of my sufferings, and that thought completely contradicted His plan for my life.

God is only GOOD. While he allows imperfection, He is incapable of being anything other than perfect.

I step back as an adult and reflect on those memories, shaking my head in wonder that I could celebrate when, over and over, there were reasons to mourn. For example, on my 17th birthday, I and about 300 friends and acquaintances attended the funeral of a good friend from church camp who died in a car accident because he was racing another car on a dangerous road. The other two in the car with him also died on impact. One of the young men's girlfriends was pregnant. That was in 1983.

In 1987 I was at my apartment when my dad called to tell me that my extremely close friend, Bryan, had been killed in a horrible car wreck. It was a Sunday, and I had skipped church. When I heard D.O.D.'s words, I felt hollow, completely shattered, and my skin stung as if I lay in a bull nettle bush. I wanted to float out of this nightmare. Bryan had been drinking with his brother's Driver's License and tried to drive back to his dorm. When the police arrived at his mom's house to give her this gut-wrenching news that they had recovered the body of a young man named Stephen*, she went to Bryan's room to tell him. Bryan wasn't there. She opened the door to Steve's* room, where he was sleeping. In minutes, she had to process the horror of thinking her oldest son had died to realize it was her youngest. They spent many years dealing with grief, guilt, shame, and immeasurable pain.

Bryan and I dated briefly, but he was inevitably my great friend. We went to church and church camp together. One summer, Bryan, his cousin Mark, my best friend Heather, and I got in major trouble for staying out WAY too late at a Lake Texoma church family camping trip over Memorial weekend. Time flew by when we were all together. Bryan and I were close, and we had a future of friendship in front of us. How could he be gone forever?

After that horrible phone call, I fell asleep a few days later. I was awoken from sleep to see Bryan at the foot of my bed. He seemed to have fog or clouds all around him. He told me, "God sent me to tell you that He will turn this dry and broken dirt you feel around you into a flowing river for your peace. He will replace your sadness with His genuine love. He is replacing the pain and torment you've already felt so many times in your short life with a fresh vision. This is peace and hope that starts now and replaces discouragement and hopelessness. So, keep your eyes focused on Him. Don't listen to the lies of the enemy. God has equipped you to take on these burdens to show others the face of Jesus, despite the heartbreak. He is real, and He wants to live in you. So don't worry

> "I now focus on improving my soul instead of working hard to improve my life. Our souls are with us for eternity, but life can leave us in a flash."
>
> *shae stewart*

about me. I'm in perfect peace because I am one with Jesus. I can't wait to show you Heaven, but you have a big job to do here first. I love you." I slept peacefully the rest of that night and woke up with a different outlook on life, God's mission for me, and how I was determined to live the rest of my days on earth, believing that God would use my suffering for good. He would use it to develop me into a better person who can love Him forever and bring others to know and love Him.

> "But that's not all! Even in times of trouble, we have a joyful confidence, knowing that our pressures will develop in us patient endurance. And patient endurance will refine our character, and proven character leads us back to hope. And this hope is not a disappointing fantasy because we can now experience the endless love of God cascading into our hearts through the Holy Spirit who lives in us!" Romans 5:3-5; The Passion Translation Bible

> "My fellow believers, when it seems as though you are facing nothing but difficulties, see it as an invaluable opportunity to experience the greatest joy that you can! You know that when your faith is tested, it stirs up the power of endurance in you. And then, as your endurance grows even stronger, it will release perfection into every part of your being until there is nothing missing and nothing lacking." James 1: 2-4; The Passion Translation Bible

In the same decade that I lost Eddie, Bryan, and Jennifer—the 80s—I lost another seven people who meant a lot to me. These deaths included a classmate in a freak accident, another three friends in alcohol-related car accidents, my maternal grandmother ten days before my birthday and two weeks before Christmas, my dad's friend died of suicide, and a family member died of pneumonia due to HIV complications.

Over the next four decades, I lost two friends to freak accidents, four to car accidents, two to motorcycle accidents, seven to alcohol or drug abuse/overdose, thirty-seven to health-related issues including cancer, my miscarriage, three friends murdered, three dying in a plane crash, two to COVID, and seven friends died of suicide (three very close friends).

I know these statistics because I recently repeated the exercise my mom asked me to complete many years ago. Once again, I received therapeutic healing by writing and praying over every name, how I knew them, how they died, and what year they left us. God reminds me to recall each of them by name so that I remember the impact they have made in my life and the lives of others. Our names carry great purpose for God, and He identifies each one of us for His Kingdom.

> LORD, he who created you, O Jacob, he who formed you, O Israel: "Fear not, for I have redeemed you; I have called you by name, you are mine." Isaiah 43 TPT

I don't write any of this to be morbid, to get pity, or sound like a negative Nellie. On the contrary, I do it as an exercise of grieving, healing, forgiving, growing, and seeking the face of Jesus through every bit of it. Counseling would have helped me through the grieving process, but I didn't know better and couldn't afford it then. However, I had the opportunity to speak a few times with one of the priests at our Episcopal church, which helped a lot. He echoed everything my mom said to me that day in 1990, and he guided me to the

Bible and back to the comfort of knowing that God would never abandon me and that I should turn to Him always, but especially when I needed Him most. I needed to feel more of Him—a tangible sign.

I took the priest's and my mom's advice and began praying. Yes, I prayed as a child, but mostly during church, at the dinner table, at bedtime, and when dealing with mean girls or a tough test. But I needed to understand how to converse with the Lord or, more importantly, be in a relationship with Him. I loved Him. I believed in Him; I had faith in every word of the Bible. There was always solace and a sense of peace when I prayed through some of the Liturgical prayers in the Book of Common Prayer. I especially connected with the Lord's Prayer, the Confession of Sin, and the Prayer of Humble Access.

> "But you are the same Lord whose character is always to have mercy." (Book of Common Prayer)

I needed mercy from my Creator. I yearned for His peace and a glimpse of His hope. My heart needed His loving arms to wrap around it to protect it from all this pain. But I didn't know how to ask Him for anything other than the tangible things in life. I had no clue how to carry on a two-way conversation with God. So, as I often do when I am desperate for solutions, I just started talking. It was often nervous chatter or asking the hundreds of questions I had for Him, like why sweet and innocent people have to suffer, if those who have died are already in Heaven, or if they have to wait until the end of the world. Through my pain, I learned to speak with God as if conversing with myself. Of course, I had to keep those conversations in my head, or people would think

I was a bit off-kilter. As I got better at talking and pausing to listen, I began to receive His responses. Sometimes it would be a simple sign that I noticed, but occasionally, I would audibly hear His word or receive an oh-so-gentle nudge that I knew was Him.

I remember driving to work many times, stressed out about the typical parts of life—traffic, kids, bills, being late, work obligations—then putting my hand in the passenger seat and simply saying out loud, "Jesus, hold my hand and tell me you're here beside me and that I don't have to go through this stress or this pain alone." Sure enough, I could feel a sense of peace whoosh throughout my body. Then, as I took a deep breath, I'd think, "Ahhh. There you are, Lord. Thank you for never leaving me. I need your grace to make it through this journey. I love you, and I trust you. Lord, your will be done. Amen."

> "Don't be pulled in different directions or worried about a thing. Be saturated in prayer throughout each day, offering your faith-filled requests before God with overflowing gratitude." Philippians 4:6-7 TPT

It was helpful to reach out to or spend time with people like my mom, best friend, boyfriend/husband, sister, and other friends or acquaintances. I'm outgoing, so it came easy to talk about the loss or losses or what I missed about the person or people I had lost, but I didn't want to come across as nagging or a victim feeling sorry for myself. I didn't want to go back to my old, pre-Junior High school, negative way of thinking. It was critical that I live out loud my main goals in life: 1. To follow Christ and 2. Make disciples (Matt. 2:18-20)

Why was I so torn? As a Christian, I know I will one day see those who were also believers in Christ, and we will spend eternity in Heaven. The words of John 3:16 run through my mind often.

> "For God so loved the world, that he gave his only Son, that whoever believes in Him should not perish but have eternal life." John 3:16 TPT

However, I was still hurting and felt confused.

Many people close to me have commented, "I don't know how you're still smiling." Even though people are generally well-intentioned, they can say very insensitive things like. "They didn't deserve to die. Why would God take them?" "She was such a good person. You know, God only takes the good ones." "God needed them more than we did." Or, "Just give it time. Time heals." By the way, time does not heal. God heals. Taking the proper steps through grief certainly helps. And if you are ever looking for something to say to a grieving person, "I can't imagine how you feel," followed by silence or a simple hug, are excellent responses. When people say hurtful things, God reminds me to "be merciful, just as your Father is merciful." (Luke 6:36)

I keep the programs of the funerals I attend. I haven't always done this but most certainly more in the past twenty years. It helps me to remember, and it helps me start the healing process by reading through them. At least 70% of the funeral programs include the 23rd Psalm. I see why, as it is comforting. It is a significant part of the prayers I say when grief hits me hard, and I especially appreciate the Passion Translation of Psalm 23:

> "Yahweh is my best friend and my shepherd. I always have more than enough. He offers a resting place for me in his luxurious love. His tracks take me to an oasis of peace near the quiet brook of bliss. That's where he restores and revives my life. He opens the right path before me and leads me along in his footsteps of righteousness so that I can bring honor to his name. Lord, even when your path takes me through the valley of deepest darkness, fear will never conquer me, for you already have! Your authority is my strength and my peace. The comfort of your love takes away my fear. I'll never be lonely, for you are near. You become my delicious feast even when my enemies dare to fight. You anoint me with the fragrance of your Holy Spirit; you give me all I can drink of you until my cup overflows. So why would I fear the future? Only goodness and tender love pursue me all the days of my life. Then, when my life is through, I'll return to your glorious presence forever with you!" Psalm 23 The Passion Translation Bible

While death is the only type of genuinely permanent loss, many other types exist. For example, most people, reading this or not, have lost someone through death, divorce, or estrangement. In addition, for example, many have faced different types of loss due to illness, finances, imprisonment, or even job. I hope the above passage brings you strength and the divine peace of Jehovah-Rapha, God who heals anyone grieving. He hopes that you pray to Him and seek Him out daily, that you are fully restored, and that your faith is strengthened in knowing that He will make us all whole again when we join Him with Jesus and the Holy Spirit in eternity.

> "Seek first his kingdom and his righteousness, and all these things will be given to you as well." Matthew 6:33 KJV

> "...Those who hope in the LORD will renew their strength. They will soar on wings like eagles; they will run and not grow weary; they will walk and not be faint." Isaiah 40:31 NIV

I recall hearing The Passion Translation version of Psalm 23 for the first time with Lori, my beautiful friend, mentor, and publisher of this book. We talked through what I would write about in my part of this pre-ordained gathering of Godly stories. I told her my subject is "Seeing the Face of Jesus in the Midst of Grief." We giggled, knowing I needed to work on the title. Next, we talked through my reservations in writing about grief because God has made it clear that my life purpose is to lift people, give away joy to others, live positively, love my neighbors, and, most importantly, make disciples (Matt. 28:19-20). In the past, I equated the emotions of grief with words like sad, depressed, lonely, worried, bitter, angry, desperate, and heartbroken, and I ran from those emotions. I was concerned that if I wrote about grief, surely people would bucket me with all those negative connotations that come to mind, which would completely conflict with my purpose. But once Lori and I discussed the reasons for this topic and shared her deep intuition that this was the subject God chose for me to write about, she said something very profound. "Honey, you've lived a life of long suffering, pain, and grief through overwhelming loss. You have lost almost 80 people who meant a lot to you, friends and family. Some were closer than others. How could you have endured all of that without it impacting your life? It's beautiful what you did with that impact, my friend. You learned to turn the glory to God. You prayed and ultimately healed through it. God is your stronghold and truly your Prince of Peace. You don't just say it; you mean it when you pray, Lord, your will be done."

I sat there in silence for an awkward amount of time. Tears ran down my face. It was at that moment that I allowed myself to accept complete healing. Jesus absolved every heartbreak from every person that I loved and lost. God held me in His hands, and I finally allowed myself to rest easy there…

And I wrote.

Prayer to God

Lord Almighty, oh, how I love and honor You! My soul thirsts to seek You, to hear You, and to feel Your presence. I know that You are the giver of peace and comfort. I ask that You wrap Your loving arms around anyone hurting for any reason, especially those who have lost someone dear to them. Remind us that we are not alone and that You promised sunshine after the rain. Bring us all the hope of Your grace and unfailing love. I ask You to wipe our tears, remove all worry, doubt, and bitterness, and fill us with Your perfect peace. Whisper to us all the words that Jesus said, "Blessed are those who mourn, for they will be comforted," as we feel grief of any type. Send us Your angels of mercy. Continue to heal our broken parts, especially our aching hearts. Help us sleep peacefully and strengthen our faith in You, Lord, so that we may all follow You closer and make disciples of people through Jesus Christ, our Lord. May the souls of all the faithful departed, through Your mercy, rest in eternal peace. And may light perpetual shine upon them. Amen.

Reflection

they will walk and not be faint

Isaiah 40:31; NIV

listen now to a love song

Lori L. Dixon, Ed.S.

"And over all these virtues (compassion, kindness, humility, gentleness, and patience) put on love, which binds them all together in perfect unity. Let the word of Christ dwell in you richly as you teach and admonish one another with all wisdom and as you sing psalms, hymns, and spiritual songs with gratitude in your hearts to God. And whatever you do, whether in word or deed, do it all in the name of the Lord Jesus, giving thanks to God the Father through him." Colossians 3:16-17 NIV

Do you hear a song, and suddenly you are transported back to that exact place and time of the first time you heard it? Does it touch you deeply? Does it bring tears to your eyes and make something stir deep inside of you? I know music does this for me and with me.

I think it all began when I was adopted and brought home for the first time. My crib was in a small room with a piano. My sister was taking piano lessons and was required (keyword required) to practice every day. I remember her playing while it was my beginning of nap time. Falling asleep to the soft melodies from that piano, sometimes with my sister singing along, was my introduction to the power and presence of music in our lives. Even though my sister rebelled daily about playing the piano for practice, I was thrilled when she did.

My whole family was music oriented! My mom and sister loved to sing, and so did I. My dad loved music but couldn't carry a tune. We loved that about him! It made us all laugh when we sang carols at the holidays, and Dad always picked "We Three Kings," and he wanted to sing it himself. I can still hear him singing "Happy Birthday" to me in his deep voice. I loved him for that every year. Mom and I sang in the choir church, and I started with solos in the elementary school choir. It was indeed a part of my greatest memories of growing up. Choirs, performance groups, and then singing and playing in bands during high school were my joys. But, most of all, singing for God was where my passions lay.

Remember the piano in my childhood bedroom that my sister would play? Well, once we moved when I was five, that piano was long gone. My sister was thrilled—no more practicing. Yet, as my interest in music grew, I leaned toward the piano. Every year for every holiday, I would request a piano, and the answer would be the same. We bought your sister one, she hated practicing, and we won't make that mistake again. By the time I was in middle school, I was already going to choir practice during the week, and guess what…my choir director's wife gave piano lessons. I shared my dilemma with her, and she felt that if I practiced what she showed me each week, she would eventually plead my case with my mom and dad. Of course, I …

The summers of the 70s, beginning at age 11, were spent in church music camps and performances, lending their way to more time with God and others who shared my feelings of faith and furthering God's messages through song. The Jesus movement was in full force, and I was glad to be part of it. We sang for God, prayed together, talked about life, and laughed about how our lives back home were so different. That was where fewer friends were open to hearing about Jesus, even though we spoke about Him everywhere.

Church was still where I felt safe and more like myself with the small group of amazing friends who attended and sang in the choir with me. One friend, Becky, loved music and went to music camp with me every summer. We talked about music and sang with her playing the guitar, which she taught me, too. She was so incredibly talented, and everyone knew it. She could write music and put her lyrics to fantastic melodies, which astounded us all. I even learned to play the guitar from her, which was my consolation instrument for not getting a piano.

Becky knew about the lessons with Mrs. Britton I was taking every week, and by this time, I was playing music and feeling good about it. Where did I practice between lessons? Everywhere! During mom's choir, I would find a piano. During Dad's meetings, I would find a piano. On vacation, I would find an old piano, and even at school, I would find a piano during classes to practice. I even drew out the keyboard on paper and carried it with me, just in case. All my friends knew I was learning piano and teaching myself most of the time. The only people who didn't know were my parents.

One particular adult choir practice night, I finished my homework and worked in a quiet room called the "parlor," where people met for smaller Bible studies, classes, or meetings. I loved this room because it had soft, comfy chairs and couches, a small kitchenette, and a piano. When the door was closed, most of the time, you couldn't hear anything going on outside the room. After finishing, I brought out a favorite piece of music I had been working on and singing with for a while. I tried to be quiet and play gently so the occasional passerby didn't hear me. I was deeply engrossed in the melodies when the door opened, and I heard a few familiar voices saying, "Choir is over." I started to pack up, and before I knew it, I was playing a few lines more. Mom was looking for me and found my choir director and his wife in the hallway.

"Who is playing the piano in the parlor tonight?" she asked them both.

Mr. and Mrs. Britton looked at each other and said, "Let's go see who it is." They knew all too well it was me!

They opened the door, and Mom walked in to see me playing the piano and singing. Her mouth dropped open, and she barely uttered a sound. Finally, I realized someone was there, and I turned around to see the Brittons and her standing there. I didn't know what to say!

On the way home, my mom asked many questions, from "How did you learn to play?" to "Where and how have you been practicing?" I excitedly answered everything she asked me because finally, I had the opportunity to show her how much I loved not only music but playing it on the guitar, clarinet (yes, that, too), voice (I had been taking lessons for years), and now...the piano. She would nod as I shared and then ask another question. I wasn't sure if I was in trouble or not at this point. Finally, she told me it was alright that I had been playing and taking lessons, but that we would be paying Mrs. Britton from here on out…out of the monies that I earned from my jobs. I was ready and willing to do anything it took to finance my passion.

Within a few months, I took complete lessons, practiced at church whenever I could, and kept up with other lessons and homework. One day the Brittons talked with my mom about finally getting me a piano for our home since I had shown her and my dad I would practice and take it seriously. My birthday was coming up, and unbeknownst to me, they all worked together to have a fabulous used piano delivered and placed in our downstairs family room. On the morning of my birthday, my parents walked me down the stairs blindfolded and let me take it off just as I stood before the new gift. As I did, my eyes gazed at my new and unbelievable gift, and I started to cry. Was it real? Was it mine? I couldn't believe it. Right then and there, I sat down with my practice music and started to play. As I pressed each key, joy grew within me. I didn't even want to stop! Guess what? I never did!

Every day after, I would go downstairs throughout the day and connect with my music and my new piano. Gone was my mom's concern about whether I would be like my sister and not want to play. The newness never wore off for me, either.

Music was always my stress relief, the much-needed escape from the pressure of school and other growing-up expectations. Before I did anything each day, music was there for me. Before a test, a date, or even a big choice, music led me closer to God, and it soothed me. After an argument, missing my dad, or feeling alone, music brought me to sit at the feet of Jesus and hear His voice.

As a therapeutic educator and administrator, I brought music and art therapy into my programs. I created ways for children with challenges and even their families to feel the strength and power of these creative outlets in their own lives.

Sometimes, I felt separated from my deep relationship with God. Whether it was an unhealthy relationship, the demands of a career, or traveling around the country as a speaker and trainer, I could feel the separation deeply within my soul. There was lacking, a hole in the harmony that music brought into my life. So, I began getting involved with music again by developing sound and movement programs, bringing me back to the Lord.

For me still, songs bring me to worship. They make me cry and lift the deeply embedded memories with my clients and me. Uplifting songs and melodies in our home or at events we create are how I communion with God. Being connected back to church through my relationship with my husband has supported my healthy "addiction" to music. He loves it, too, so our home is always filled with the songs of either eras gone by or our faith and love for God.

Music grounds me and brings me closer to God. Part of the story I hadn't shared with you yet, is when I left Illinois with my parents at 18 years old to move to Florida, I wasn't around to pack up my room or my items from my childhood. I trusted they were lovingly doing that all for me. When I finally got to Florida and started seeing all the boxes filling the new house's garage, I thought things would be fine. Then, my thoughts changed drastically. I walked into the house and through each room, seeing where Mom envisioned everything would go. There was a new bedroom set for me, the twin set of my childhood in the spare room for the guests who would visit us, and my dad's new desk and bookcases in the next bedroom to create a study for him and Mom. There was new furniture in the family room and our living room furniture for the new room. I loved the gorgeous dining room set filled with my favorite family, antique dishes, and glasses showing through the glass on the front. Things looked beautiful and ready for us to start a new life here together. Mom and Dad still had the same bedroom furniture since they got it when they first married. The newest room was the screened-in lanai with outdoor furniture. I walked through carefully, ooo-ing and ahhhing all the way.

Then, I realized my piano wasn't in any of the rooms. I rechecked the garage to see if I had missed it. It wasn't there. My heart sank, and my chest began to fill up with the reaction of grief. My breath quickened, and I started to cry. Not just a little weeping, an ugly cry. Mom and Dad couldn't console me for what seemed like an eternity. I sat back on the lanai, listening to the birds singing and trying to calm down my hurt and loss.

Mom was the first one to speak, and she tried to explain why they had left my piano. The discussion included:

- The humidity.
- The long transport trip.
- The risks involved in protecting it.
- The space for it in the house.

Finally, she reassured me that it went to a new church looking for a piano and that they felt I would feel good about that decision. It made all complete sense to my head but not my heart. How would I release stress now in college, in a new city, and looking for new friends and relationships?

Mom and Dad also shared that I would only be with them for a few more years before my career and a new place may be in my immediate future. Oh, well. I gave in to what had happened and knew time was changing, life was shifting, and I had to learn to adjust differently.

Life went on, yet I never stopped praying for a piano. I dated someone with a baby grand piano and began reacquainting myself with the beautiful keys and melodic sounds. However, once that experience between us was over, I moved on, never releasing the fact that one day, a piano would enter my life and music would fill the space.

After I married my husband, we cultivated a very special relationship with our neighbors, Rob and Kelly, and their sweet girls. They have become like family; we have watched their girls grow from infants to young women. Recently, as they were moving to a nearby house, they chatted with us at dinner. They were trying to sell some items that wouldn't fit in the new home. One item was the family piano! It was Kelly's great-grandmother's, and both girls had learned to play because it was in their home. Yes, it was well-loved and ready to be moved to a new owner to love it.

"God is in now in each note I am working on playing again."

lori l. dixon

The girls were now playing keyboards and singing, and we loved going to their plays and concerts. We knew this piano was a part of their life. Kelly and Rob told us how the person that was to buy it didn't call back or set anything up with them. Now they had to move and figure something out within days. I looked at Art…he knew the look…could it be that our best friend's piano could be the "one" God wanted me to have? After a quick conversation, they decided to gift me the piano, and it was "moved" by two piano-moving men by rolling it down the street three houses to our front door. Now, it resides in our home with a beautiful corner for me to walk by every day and touch, thanking God for the reminder that He is always watching for the right time for things to come to us.

God is in now in each note I am working on playing again. I kept all my sheets and book music that were my favorites, too. It is a new perfect therapeutic practice for me, as I have the autoimmune challenge of rheumatoid arthritis. Do you think God knew the timing was perfect for Rob, Kelly, the girls, AND me? I believe it was. God's timing is always excellent.

One of my favorite books of music is the Love Song album from an obscure band in the 70s. They weren't Christians when they started, and under the guidance of the original band owner, Chuck Girard, they gave their lives to Christ and began writing and performing Christian music. The music sits on my piano, which is one of the things I am working on playing again.

Recently, my husband and I went to see the Jesus Revolution movie because we lived in that era, and I performed much of the Christian music in the 70s and early 80s. As we watched the movie and giggled, pointing out the cars, the clothing, the messages, and the music, it was a pure reminder to us of our growing-up lives. When the band began playing on stage at the church in California, they were introduced as LOVE SONG. I almost fell out of my movie seat. I looked at Art, and I started tearing up. God was in control! He reminded me of my life and returned to IN HIM! Over the last two years, I have deepened my walk with Christ and been "recalled" by him to serve in new ways. The group started playing my very favorite song, A LOVE SONG. That was the exact song I had been practicing. I began to cry and sing quietly with the band… "listen now to a love song…."

I share the beautiful and heartfelt words with you.

A Love Song[1]

by Chuck Girard and Jessie Johnston

Lend an ear to a love song
Oooh, a love song
Let it take you. Let it start
What can you hear in a love song?
If you can feel it,
Then you're feelin' from the heart

All the emotions and true feelings of life are what music of love is about
If you are listening with peace in your heart and no doubt
So listen now to a love song
If you can hear it
We will never be apart

A Love Song for God… isn't that exactly how it feels and sounds?

Music brings us back into communion. Releases all the challenges of the day and gives them to Jesus…I honor him and thank him.

Did you know King David wrote worship music to God before he was King and after? Did you know how many songs he wrote? 150! Can you imagine singing everything to God as you commune with him? I can! That is how God and I, most of the time, talk to each other and where I hear him so strongly. As a seer, visionary, and prophet, I bring forth God's voice for me and others in their journey. But MY time

---

[1] ©1972 Love Song album www.chuckgirard.com

with God is precious! Words and melodies of songs heal me in so many ways. I know they do for many of you, too.

Remember how God walks with you and talks with you every day. Even when we think he isn't listening to things as small as the desire to have a piano again, he does! Never stop believing!

Reflection

put on love

Colossians 3:16-17

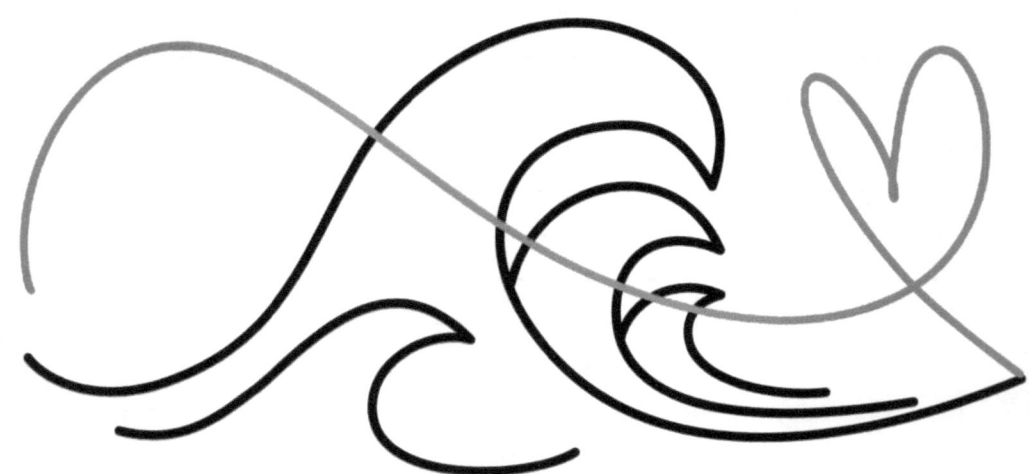

the glory steps

Step Into the Word

Lulite Ejigu

"And the priests were not able to stand to serve because of the cloud, for the Glory of the Lord had filled the house of God." 2 Chronicles 5:14

"I will send you such a blessing in the sixth year that the land will yield enough for three years. While you plant during the eighth year, you will eat from the old crop and continue to eat from it until the harvest of the ninth year comes in." Leviticus 25:21-22

Calm Down, Cloudiness Is God's Glory

As Mahatma Ghandi says, "There is more to life than increasing its speed." The seasons have an appointed time so let me begin my story on the journey today at my current time, "year five." Soon, you will understand what that looks like, but for now, let's go back to my previous "year three."

Year three was exciting, confusing, and a great year of bravery for me. I was coming out of some extensive years of change, as I left the only career I knew without a plan. I began new work projects globally in Ethiopia, gave birth to my son, came out of the hospital with COVID at the height of the virus craze, and that was just the year prior.

Like many of us, our lives were spun around a few times in the laundry machine of life, but if my life didn't have enough ups and downs, I got an intense urge to jump into politics. Yes, I know you are wondering, "h no, why politics?" I could have shifted into advocacy, humanitarian work, and even strategy for another candidate, which would make sense to me. But instead, even though I was not too fond of politics and had no political work experience, I was hyper-aware of the outrageous happenings around us.

What did I do? I brought it to God as my questions and humorous responses quickly started to turn to conviction. Finally, I asked God if this was really what I was supposed to do, and He showed up and answered. Not only in a bible study I was taking at the time, but right when I got the most straightforward message from God, it was found in a missed text on my phone saying, "Hey, like seriously, I think you should run." There was the only confirmation I needed.

Yet, I immediately felt the panic, the heat from my body almost creating a sweat as I had just returned from a jog. It just got serious and honest. My passive jokes with others were no longer just something I could giggle about and secretly desire. I was now getting a very LOUD ping. I took a moment in my bedroom in silence, knowing this was a "calling" from God I needed to carry. I immediately felt the weight of this new mantle given to me. I began researching for the next two months to see how feasible this was.

Let's say everything pointed to NOT NOW, but God said the ultimate phrase, "I am here." With the excitement of waiting on a miracle and knowing the type of "moving mountains" kind of miracles God can do, I was anxiously following Him. The massive journey for digesting the knowledge required of public servant life and what campaigning looks like began. I often had to say to myself, "I am going to run for the U.S. Congress!"

Running for office is daunting, even when you are savvy about the process, have numerous individuals on your campaign team, and when prepared, statements come naturally around the needs of a community and its constituents. Yet, through all the networking, meetings, interviews, and the average person on the street, I would have to answer and defend my every thought, not to mention the famous question, "why should I vote for you"? Honestly, every day I wondered, what was I going to tell them? Did I know the correct answer? My first thoughts were that at least I would speak the ugly reality, so I responded, "I am going to fight for the truth"! Let's say I got many blank stares and follow-up questions, but those I spoke with understood my Spirit of service and gave me grace in my words. Thank God! The truth is I never thoroughly answered that question confidently. I was still searching for a precise answer that didn't push me into political talking points, and yet still FULLY respond to the simple but tricky question.

The initial step on my official mission was learning how to run a campaign for U.S. Congress with no base knowledge in less than two months. Where did I begin? I researched the essential dates and requirements I would need. To my surprise, the first data point I found was the registration date, which happened to be my son's birthday, and to me, that was a confirmation from God to be courageous.

Then, the following reminder of a God moment was as I looked up congressional districts. I saw neighborhoods and areas repeatedly reflecting my son's unique name. All the confirmations are too many to list, yet all are part of the journey. How could I walk through the cloudiness of running a congressional campaign? As I would walk through the challenges of explaining to political consultants that God needed me to do this at this time, and in this way, you can imagine their replies and even strange glances. During this experience, I pondered on this verse, and it made me better understand where I was and realize what this season was all about:

> "And the priests could not stand to serve because of the CLOUD, for the glory of the Lord had filled the house of God."
> 2 Chronicles 5:14

Confusion and conviction can often feel the same on the surface because they both make you ask, "Am I doing the right thing?" and even "is this truly the right step God wants me to take?" The critical difference, I have found, is that when you are in conviction, God has already ordained every step, and you already have the directions, however, you must surrender to the path.

Yet, we must understand that God reveals them for us, one by one, in His divine timing. If you were like me and had every step in the process, you would hit fast forward and miss the nuances of His perfection for us. Therefore, in every experience God allows us to walk into, we must remember that the cloud is one step in Glory.

These are what I would call "glory steps," where the knowledge that we will arrive at the destination if we lean into the direction of God in His truth. We cannot miss our goal if we walk with God. He never fails. As we are on this path, we are divinely supported and are on the winning team. It is written in the scriptures that we are to move from Glory to Glory, which means every single step or experience builds on each other. When embracing the Glory, you begin to see that the cloudiness is the Glory of God filling the space and covering the whole path only for us to focus on Him and what He has placed gently in our hands to do.

"I am the daughter of a King, and my steps are numbered and anointed for His Kingdom."

lulite ejigu

Glory steps give me insight for when I beg God for wisdom or feel alone and the world tells me I am not worthy of doing something. God supports me to remember… I am the daughter of a King, and my steps are numbered and anointed for His Kingdom.

Little did I know my most significant "glory steps" could never be skipped as the location and surroundings were the ingredients I needed for each breakthrough. This gives me a sense of bravery and courage as I remember that all of these steps I have taken in my life are needed to arrive at my appointed destination.

We, as women, are genuinely aware of how God gives us this immense ability to create another human life; in that, we are reminded that we are co-creators with Him. While pregnant, a woman shares her body while pregnant to grow, safely carry, and nurture a baby. This miraculous experience increases our awareness of everything we consume, do, and even think. In God's magnificent creation principle, however, there are subtractions too, and if we aren't paying attention, we only focus on those things we have had to subtract, not on what is multiplied. Therefore, we must be present and know that our STEPS toward our destination are vital as we walk with God in all that Glory.

Following God's "GPS"

In all these life experiences, would it be wonderful to have an instruction manual or directions to reach our destiny? Literally highlighting glory step by glory step, preferably! What if that's precisely what we have, but instead, we continue staring at the address or destination? It can get frustrating for those who love our navigation system but hate when it disconnects or redirects us, forcing us to take U-turns and extend our routes. If you are like me, my most significant focus to attend to while driving somewhere is the "estimated time of arrival" or ETA update.

One Bible story that reminds me of the power in God's GPS is Moses and his search for the promised land. Imagine it with a view of it in today's times. He starts so well on God's super bullet train out of Egypt, I mean, there was no faster or more efficient path than the Red Sea splitting, but then the re-routing begins. The promised land was only supposed to be less than a couple of weeks journey, yet it took them forty years because they were going in circles. When we look back at the reasons for the delay, we see it was due to the people complaining and ignoring the navigation of God's GPS.

We know we aren't any different than the children of God from thousands of years ago, so it is important we don't make the same mistakes and miss or delay our promises. I knew I needed to look at what directions could be a guideline that God gave us similar to a step-by-step process. It suddenly hit me and I realized God had detailed descriptions of Creation down to what was designed and planned for each day. I knew this was an important revelation and I said to myself, "You are made in the image and likeness of God so you must be a co-creator." These day-by-day creation plans and steps were the directions to His Glory. As this truth became evident, my excitement created a burst of energy! I couldn't wait to study the seven-day Creation story as outlined in Genesis and get the "glory steps". These precious steps are our life's walk and purpose for the Kingdom. Let's put this in God's GPS and see what directions are given.

1. ***Turn RIGHT into TRUTH***: Light is truth, truth is knowledge, and wisdom leans us into Glory. If the light reflects off light, God says he is the lamp at our feet, lighting up our steps along the path. It is also written that we are to move from Glory to Glory. The start of any divine calling or mission must first seek out the truth. For me, this started with searching all the promises in God's word that supported my conviction and getting in alignment with foundational truth. On the days you can't see, God's promises help validate the

direction and confirm that this is the journey. The first step is getting on the road, even with the clouds in your way.

"And this Living Expression's creative inspiration made all things, for nothing exists apart from Him! A fountain of life was in him, for his life is light for all Humanity. And this light never fails to shine through the darkness—Light that night could not overcome." John 1:3-5 TPT

2. ***Head North with your Eyes Toward Heaven:*** Divine promises and destinations will always elevate us as it is ordered and established in heaven first. We find the north star prepared by God through leaning into what best brings joy into our Spirit. I left the only career I knew this season to move closer to what would give me satisfaction. The hardest void I've had to fill along the journey. Yet, with that one opening, I planted over a dozen seeds that immediately began producing fruit in my life. This "glory" step may require you to take the exit lane and move away from the traffic jam. You may even be forced to focus and look toward heaven during this time as God will prepare what turns are next.

3. ***Yield ahead and deepen ROOTS:*** As you yield to Him, you deepen your relationship. Surrendering to His profound words will align you to grow toward your purpose and mission. Like the trees that can rise higher and with more stability based on the deeper and more intricate the root system is below ground. More "glory steps" will appear as you grow and yield to Him.

"As you yield to the vibrant life and power of the Holy Spirit, you will abandon the craving for your self-life… But when you yield to the life of the Spirit, you will no longer be living under the law but soaring above it." Galatians 5: 16, 18 TPT

Have you ever noticed how God uniquely placed the seed for a fruit tree within the fruit itself? This is a perfect picture of what He does in each of us. He carefully and intricately places the seed that will produce an outpouring of fruitfulness and further seed development deep down in us. The root system is systematically part of the growth and can only be built by complete surrender and fellowship, walking hand in hand with God. It requires "stepping" inward as the truths from God (GPS) give us the clarity we need to find our direction. With the lessons of this wisdom through "glory steps," I found such peace and understanding toward revealing and writing my vision. This step requires finetuning and shaping our vision, and it can be a journey of challenges and obstacles. Yet, remember, you are stepping in "glory steps" with the creator of your vision and purpose.

4. ***Speed Up:*** You are coming into a season of new growth and order in your life. This scripture speaks to the movement and action these "glory steps" will provide.

"For wisdom is more moving than any motion: she passeth and goeth through all things because of her pureness." Wisdom of Solomon 7:24, Apocrypha

You did the deep work and slowed down, but now it's time to organize your efforts with discernment and press in. The seasons change, just like seasons in our own lives. They blend into one another first. This "glory step" looked like I was going backward. We may see snow in spring or increased warm temperatures in winter. Although these instances may cause alarm they are only glitches, however, they are essential resets holding divine purpose. Stay calm, and be in the flow God is providing for you and you will glide into the next season.

5. ***STAY straight, destination up ahead***: This IS the time. Maintaining this endurance for the road may test our faith however this strengthens our wisdom. In this place, we need to be steady and stay the course.

> "Forgetting what is behind and straining toward what is ahead, I press on toward the goal to win the prize for which God has called me heavenward in Christ Jesus." Philippians 3:14 NIV

You feel the Glory and can even be engulfed in it. I am in this step right now, and I am noticing that although the cloudiness is getting thicker, I am getting clearer. My journey has been to find and embrace clarity. During this season, the most precise picture I have is The Glory of the King. This awe fills my nose like a fresh breeze, yet the Father's crown blinds me with its brilliant glow. I bow my head and close my eyes, and still light remains. God's power is present. I am putting two hands on the wheel. I acknowledge His presence and move slowly forward.

6. ***Arrival:*** You arrived and all in God's perfect timing! You will now be first in line, first place, the head and not the tail. It is time to store your harvest and count God's outstanding provision. This is the multiplication of all sacrificed, the birth after the toiling labor. Open the door and receive!

7. ***Stay parked:*** every piece of wisdom starts from our example, and God showed us that resting and taking time to see the good in His Creation and the journey was the most critical part of all the directions. So recline your seat and enjoy the heavens as they celebrate with you today.

"Here's the one thing I crave from God, the only thing I seek above all else. I want to live with him every moment in his house, beholding the marvelous beauty of Yahweh, filled with awe, delighting in his Glory and grace." Psalm 27:4 TPT

Not to state the obvious but it is clear in these directions just like the directions we load on our GPS daily, that we can't just skip a step and still arrive at our destination. Navigation through life is essential. There can be re-routing or "short-cuts" that we may believe may get us there faster, but our free will and "detour" choices force us into destinations that were not part of the plan. We must remember that God's GPS, promises, and satellite vision is better than our limited visibility.

If we take how God created the universe in less than a week, but go back and see what was created each day, we can see a theme. It was no surprise that God not only has provision for what to do but also a common practice of when not 'to do' and just REST. No matter where we are in our journey, we can be encouraged that surely the earth is our inheritance.

The Seven Years

I started this story by letting you know I am in my own "year five" and sharing the "Glory steps" I have walked with you. Through this current journey, I remembered this exciting promise from God:

> "I will send you such a blessing in the sixth year that the land will yield enough for three years. While you plant during the eighth year, you will eat from the old crop and continue to eat from it until the harvest of the ninth year comes in." Leviticus 25:21-22

Realizing my ETA, I am in my fifth step and at the cusp of my overabundant harvest. There is still much to do, and I am still determining all the experiences that may arise on this road prepared ahead. What I do know is I finally found the answer to my most-asked campaign question, "Why should I vote for you"? My answer is you shouldn't. You should vote for YOU. The YOU that was molded by the God of the universe. Vote for what shakes your core, what excites you, and of course, what brings in healing. Like the fruit tree's seed placed within the fruit itself, I found the answers were never about anything outside myself. Walking with the holy spirit is the seed and it provides me with a constant source of solutions. We need only to tap in. I guess it was always within us all along and the solution can be found within the problem itself.

Wisdom Concealed and REVEALED

You may still need an ETA on your personal "promised land." Or ask, "How long does each step take, and where am I on this journey?"

I do have an answer, but doesn't it all just depend? However, for those in present suffering, be encouraged that future "glory steps" are just ahead for you!

> "Our present sufferings are not worth comparing with the Glory that will be revealed in us." Romans 8:18 NIV

Like our ancestors complaining in the wilderness to Moses, these moments we suffer can't even touch the surface of how perfect our place is in the Kingdom. He has stored and concealed great treasures in our hearts waiting for us to unveil them.

> "It is the Glory of God to conceal a matter; to search out an issue is the Glory of kings." Proverbs 25:2 NIV

The Glory cannot be revealed if it was never first concealed, and that is a part of God's magnificent designs. It requires us to take the "GLORY steps" to find the truth and follow the path. Each action may be cloudy, challenging, or even sometimes seem pointless; however, they are divinely necessary. I may not have won these past elections, but there is no doubt now that it was always a marathon, and I will surely WIN the race.

Remember:

- God is a God of order and sees His demand as perfect.
- His declaration may be easy to follow if you align with Him and honor His purpose path.
- Seven appears to us as God's holy number and even a core truth in Creation, now and then.
- God detailed His blueprint for navigation within the sacred words in His scriptures of creation.

To answer the pressing question of "where am I on the ETA?", let me dare to clarify! In conclusion, if the God of gods that created all creation, is a God of order, and detailed that order to us then that is a blueprint. The "glory steps" is a seven-step blueprint foundation, the same foundation that was good enough for the building of the universe, then it should be good enough for us. However, whether it's seven years or seven days keep your eyes on the compass, because you may just miss your turn when you're focusing on the ETA and not the directions right in front of you.

Prayer to God

Thank you, Lord, for the great truths you have revealed in us this day. Thank you for being our shield, protecting our every step as David didn't carry a shield for protection in battle, knowing you were all around him like a cloud of Glory, so be that in our lives. Forgive us of all our sins and lack of wisdom at times, as we know you are just and faithful to forgive. Remind us of our majestic power and authority as, after all, we are the sons and daughters of the KING. Amen!

Reflection

patience on the walk

Lori L. Dixon, Ed.S.

You may not have the patience to read a long story today, so I wrote this one shorter for you.

Don't we feel this way much of the time these days? Everything is a rush, time seems to be fleeting, and we must have more patience sometimes to make it through the day, with increased expectations with work, family, friends, community, outside activities, our health, and even our faith. After COVID, life shifted. We had to learn about patience in different ways. It reminded us to slow down, realize our relationships, place more importance on our health, see the depth of connection in our lives, and more about patience.

Many moms struggled with working from home, having a house filled with children and even a significant other, or being alone. Working from home and supporting our children in their online school, we created new ways of being fully present and ON throughout the day. No wonder why anxiety and depression were on an increased amount. It was overwhelming to many, to say the least.

Churches, for the first time, closed their doors to people. Services were held online, and even bible studies halted because life was overwhelming for us. So how could you find a quiet corner to do a bible study when caring for your and your family's focus and on-task behaviors?

How did we survive? Once we pushed through our resistance to the new increased responsibilities, we learned to have moments of EASE and found our rhythm throughout the day. We learned to slow down and be patient in everything we were doing. We found what was important to us in our situation. We adapted and figured out the importance of relationships again. We called each other more; we reached out and checked on those who needed to hear a kind word or a reassuring voice.

My clients discuss patience and struggle with it in almost every session I have with them. It is a human challenge, and every age in life is learning it in their interactions, situations, and relationships with others, including themselves. So you can imagine how COVID was an even more significant part of our conversations.

It was a turning in our life. Realizing patience in all, trusting, and believing that God was working on us and supporting the next steps in our life, gave us peace and, sometimes, when we allowed ourselves, comfort. Life became essential to us again. Caring and compassion increased, and so did prayer!

It is said that "patience is the capacity to tolerate challenges and delays without getting upset. Most of us would love more patience in our lives, but it's not always easy" (Compassion International, 2023).

Jesus was the most remarkable example of patience. He knew it was a problematic characteristic for people, so he exhibited it in almost every story, lesson, and experience with him. What a teacher! He shared, explained, and modeled patience in every way for us to see it lived out with his words and actions.

The Bible tells us that patience is a by-product of increased wisdom. Notice how we, as individuals, continually desire to grow in our wisdom and receive the quieter outcomes of patience. It is true that with age come wisdom and patience. The scripture continues to tell us that LOVE is patient and that we should wait on the Lord, and in our waiting, patience is received within us.

> "So, don't lose your bold, courageous faith, for you are destined for great reward. You need the strength of endurance (patience) to reveal the poetry of God's will, and then you receive the promise in full." Hebrews 10:36 The Passion Translation

As I read the numerous scriptures where God and Christ are sharing the lesson and learning of patience, the pattern of the instruction and increased expectation is evident. We are to be maturing in HIM, not reacting like children after He presents the opportunities for us. God is our Abba, Father, and his teaching is given in such ways to have us become the leaders of the Kingdom of God on earth. He wants us to take our rightful place next to him again and to walk in authority and direction. How can we do that without patience?

You may have heard that you, "Never pray for more patience. God may answer your prayer and give you a reason to need more." God gives us the desires of our hearts. If He feels you need the fruit of patience to grow and bloom in your life, you will receive more opportunities to practice it. We know God is genuinely patient with us in everything we do and say. We are HIS children, and His patience is always present in our learning.

"If He feels you need the fruit of patience to grow and bloom in your life, you will receive more opportunities to practice it."

lori l. dixon

Patience increases in the situations and lessons of our ever-changing lives. My adult children learn patience with their children every day. Children are an excellent source of pushing us to understand their independence and emotional growth. Every age gives us a new pattern of this growth, and patience is necessary, not needed, but necessary.

We grow in our faith, hope, and love by learning patience with our children as they grow.

Those with whom we have been responsible for "care" require our utmost patience and compassion. The Church at Thessalonica received direction in Paul's letters while he could not be with them. He was still in "care" of them and their upbringing in the way of Christ. Sometimes those we guide and mentor fall into old habits or actions that are not "of God." We struggle with it, just as Paul did.

"For we remember before our God and Father how you put your faith into practice, how your love motivates you to serve others, and how unrelenting is your hope-filled patience in our Lord Jesus Christ." 1 Thessalonians 1:3 TPT

Reflection

how unrelenting is your hope-filled patience

1 Thessalonians 1:3

open heart

Our Greatest Strength Is Love

Judy Cochrane

I peered out the airplane window as we descended into Tucson, Arizona's magnificent mountain range. Typically, a surge of excitement is felt when visiting this city. But today, it just reminded me of the recent losses of my stepfather and, six months later, my biological father. My heart ached for the two men who raised me in different but profound ways. Unfortunately, I couldn't see either of them in person before they passed, which is why I was high tailing it out to be with my mom before her open-heart surgery, scheduled for the following day. She is 84, and I wouldn't risk not seeing her one last time.

My sister, Cary, who lives in Tucson, picked me up from the airport. I stood curbside for only a minute in the cool 40-

degree desert weather as I studied the gray skies, which were abnormal for this time of year. The forecast showed no sign of sun for the next two weeks. I shrugged it off, knowing I'd be cooped up in a hospital for the next few days. There would surely be no time for basking in the sun, going on desert hikes, or gazing at the hot pink, gold, and orange sunsets that Arizona is known for.

On the drive to my mom's, as always, my eyes gazed outside as I was flooded with years of memories. This wasn't just a place I visited. This is where my husband and I predominantly raised our three kids. For 20-plus years, it was our home, filled with experiences and moments in time that formed not just me but our entire family. We took a right-hand turn and passed the bank where I sat years ago when our account was closed due to going from 35 million to food stamps—a story I wrote about while still living here. So much good, bad, and ugly had unfolded. Yet all of it served us right, but in a divine way. In the end, a lot was gained in losing our American dream. The truth is, lessons were learned, and I could finally feel grateful for it all.

Without hesitation or a hello, as I crossed the threshold of my mom's apartment at The Hacienda in Sabino Canyon Retirement Home, my mom exclaimed, "I cannot frigging believe it! I went to pre-op today, and I tested positive for COVID! I told the surgeon I have zero symptoms and am demanding this surgery NOT be canceled!" She stomped across the room, throwing her hands up in the air. "This has been canceled and rescheduled already! I am done! I want this over with!"

I had always admired her fortitude in the face of adversity, but I wanted to lighten things by saying, "Wow, Mom! That's some news. So, what you're saying is no hug? Fine with me. I didn't come here to get COVID," I said while my sister and I broke into laughter.

I offered her an air hug, and she returned the gesture.

I knew my mom was strong, but I also knew her well enough to know that validation was in order. "But seriously though, I don't blame you, Mom. You've been through a lot over the last couple of years. Loss of your husband [my stepfather], Bill, and then Dad, and then your colon surgery last March were all devastating. You are a trooper. Let's keep the faith and trust that all is in order and that they allow this surgery to proceed tomorrow."

After dinner and when we were all alone, I watched her go about packing her bags, cleaning out her purse, and organizing sets of keys for me to easily enter the apartment, her car, and the mailbox. She shared passcodes for her phone and laptop and reviewed the call lists that I had and that Cary was in charge of. While I was unpacking, she stepped into the room and sat at her desk. Then, she swiveled around in her chair to look at me.

While leaning over my bag, I sensed her and turned to look back at her. It was one of those moments when nothing was said, but everything was said. I teared up but knew not to start crying. She wasn't a crier. She was raised by a mother who rarely shed a tear and often hid her emotions. For me, growing up with a mother like that was both beneficial and sometimes tricky. I, along with my sister, are Pisces (for those of you who pay attention to horoscope signs), known for *people who wear their hearts on their sleeves*. My brother, Johnny, is a truth-teller who speaks straight from the heart. We laugh about the earlier days when my mom would say, "You guys are too sensitive; toughen up." It was often the kick in the ass we needed, but today it felt like our turn to say to her, "You don't have to be so tough, Mom. It's fair to be afraid. We have you covered."

It was becoming clear to me that someone who would be literally cracked open, placed on heart and lung machines, and likely face all the things (elevated emotions) that can come from open heart surgery was now appearing to be the luckiest woman alive. Having two sensitive daughters and a son with a heart, all of which could individually and together hold space for the fear, the pain to come, any unknown setbacks, any sadness (new or old), or any residual anxiety that could surface, placed her in good hands, with us.

I broke our silence by picking up a picture of my stepdad, Bill. She smiled. "I miss him," I said. She nodded in silence. I could see the hurt in her eyes, but I didn't push her to talk about him. She missed him so much, especially in times like these. My primary role tonight was to keep her nervous system calm, so I stuck to the plan.

She pointed to binders stacked on the closet shelves behind me.

"The power of attorney, the trust, my fully paid cremation papers, etc., are all in those binders. Cary knows of all this, just wanted you to help her if…"

I interjected, "Okay, Mom. Got it."

"I know I am in good hands with you kids," she said.

"Yep. You are also in the good hands of another." I smiled.

She nodded in agreement and shared, "At church, they prayed for me. It felt good. I don't like that attention, as you know, but I welcomed it. They are sincere people."

I replied, "Well, I don't want to get preachy, but let's go over prayer for a moment. Remember how we did this for your colon surgery, and what they thought was cancer turned out to be a miracle that it was not? They even canceled your oncologist appointment! I'm still in awe. So let us remember to pray with a grateful heart AS IF the request has already been granted. Imagine yourself in recovery, delightfully surprised by how well you are doing. How quickly you are released. How uneventful the recovery is. How soon you are back on your feet. And how amazing it feels to be hanging out with all your friends again. Oh, and I pray that Dr. Bose and the anesthesiologist, nurses, techs, and all that you will be in the hands of have a beautiful night of sleep and eat well tonight and tomorrow while they shine bright as they work on you and around you. Amen… and it is done."

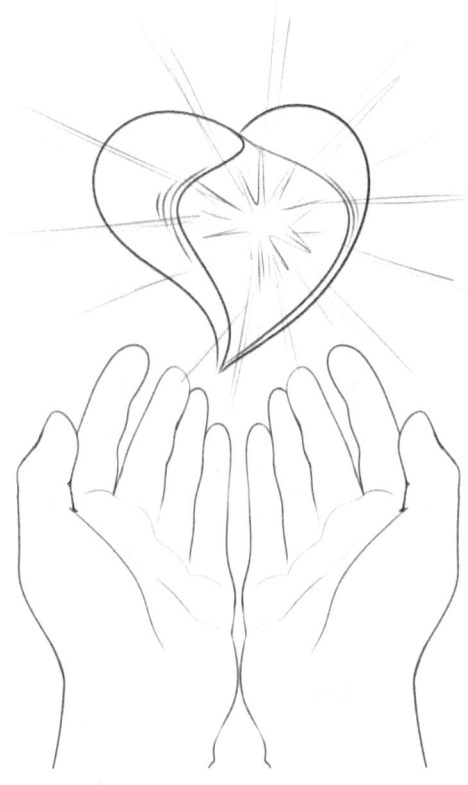

She replied, "And it is done."

"And I trust he'll send the angels," I added.

"Ah. Yes. I have been praying to my angels. A lot," she said, looking over at Bill's photo.

When I awoke the following day, I reflected on my past studies that had helped me through more challenging times in my life. For the past three decades, I'd studied meditation, spirituality, religion, hypnotherapy, NLP (neuro-linguistic programming), yoga, self-awareness, self-development, alternative and holistic healing methods, and the power of the mind and energy in our bodies to both harm and heal ourselves. Yet, in sharing this with others, I have found one bottom line: One must have an *open heart* in seeking truth, practicing faith, and trusting in God's hand in our lives, regardless of circumstances or conditions.

> "Opening our hearts is a heart-surrender process in which we are gently carried rather than buried."
> —Nicole Faith

While still in bed, I basked in the curiosity of the play on words, and I started to fall in love with the symbolism of my mom's open-heart surgery. The aneurysm was on her aorta. The aorta is the body's largest artery and carries blood from the heart to the circulatory system. Without this, we live with dis-ease. Similarly, without an open heart, we are at dis-ease with ourselves, others, and God.

This operation had become an opportunity for us to connect. Coming together with open hearts was another blessing, as we could lean on each other's strengths. My aunt Judy (my namesake) lived in Tucson in the winter months and was right there by all our sides too. It was a special treat for me to spend time with her and laugh together. I hadn't had that much time with her since I was a kid. And it was quality time. Why? Because our hearts were open.

> "It's all just a big love contest, and I never lose."
> —Hafiz

I also saw the connection to how all circumstances can divinely serve us right, even if it's seemingly bad news. When we look back at both the heartbreaks in our life and the heart-opening moments, they tend to not only be our dominant memories, but they are the lessons and gifts that end up being our greatest blessings.

As I continued to reflect, the symbolism of an open heart grew, and I could see how this fine gold thread ran through all of us and our lives. Open hearts are the only ones that can connect us, and a closed heart is the only one that will isolate us from one another.

> "So I'm asking you, my friends, that you be joined together in perfect unity—with one heart, one passion, and united in one love. Walk together with one harmonious purpose, and you will fill my heart with unbounded joy." Philippians 2:2 TPT

The following morning, I watched my mom lie on the hospital bed while being prepped for surgery. Then, finally, the nurse said, "Okay, Judy, it's time to let her go. We are ready for surgery now."

Her words, "Let her go," startled me. I locked eyes with my mom, and I wasn't sure if she heard it the way I had. Of course, they had her entirely distracted with tubes, taping, etc. But it made me think. Was I ready to let her go? Yes and no. I then sensed the peace that came from this open heart of mine.

Even though I was wildly vulnerable, I loved her with my open heart, which felt like magnificent strength. There was not one more ounce of love that I was holding back. I was all in. I felt peace and appreciation as I re-examined our imperfect life together. My heart felt full. If she was going to depart, she had done her part. She was my mother. She loved me, and I loved her. As a mother of three, I can only hope to show up for my children with an open heart, allowing them to feel what I felt that day as they wheeled her away.

The surgeon convinced me that staying in the lobby for 5+ hours was unnecessary. So instead, they arranged to have a nurse call me with occasional updates. He explained it will be at critical points: "when we open her up, when we put her lungs and heart on a machine, and when they repair the aneurysm."

I returned to her apartment and turned the radio to 70's soft rock. The first and second calls came, but much time passed with no call. I checked my phone numerous times for the next two hours. She had made it through the first hurdles, but a call on the aneurysm being repaired was crucial, and if she stayed under for too long at her age, things were getting riskier by the minute.

Distracting myself, I went outside to visit my stepdad's memorial cactus garden, which he had planted before passing. The unexpected sunshine hit the tops of my shoulders as I looked up to a deep blue sky with puffy white clouds that showed promise of a rich sunset tonight. Sitting on his bench, I sighed, closed my eyes, and prayed again. *Thank you for this day.* I heard a flutter in the mesquite trees and noticed a hummingbird hovering nearby. Even though that was an expected sight here, that was also a sign of my stepdad, Bill. Then, I saw a bright red cardinal swoop past me and nestle onto a mesquite tree branch. That was an unexpected sight this time of year. A cardinal always represented my grandma, my mom's mother.

As I was about to express gratitude for these signs, I heard the song "The Rose" wafting from my mom's apartment.

That's a song I always sang with my Aunt Judy to and for my stepdad, and we even sang it at his celebration of life. My mouth dropped as I headed back to confirm. I touched my heart and whispered, "Hi, Bill. Thank you for being here."

Directly behind my mom's apartment is a magnificent hill with 14 prayer stations called The Stations of the Cross. The convent next door houses six nuns, all elderly. Their church, St. Thomas, created the path up this hill for all their parishioners and the general public. Having never explored this hill before, I took off. I started at station one and made my way up. I remained present with each step, not only because it was extremely steep in some areas but also because I pondered how much holy water had soaked into the desert floor in these parts. Each station had mementos, stones, and crystals that others had left behind. I had my prayers covered today, so I prayed for theirs to be answered.

At the top, perched in pure white cement, enormous statues of Mary, Joseph, and Jesus stood like fortresses. The silence up here was deafening. I pulled my hood over my head to break the whipping wind and angled myself toward the sun to feel it warm my face. I looked up and around. From here, you could see all of Tucson in 360 degrees. The vast, snow-capped mountain range hugged the entire city. I glanced at my iPhone again, wondering why I wasn't hearing from the nurse.

I stood in front of the large cross, which towered above me, feeling the force of spirit all around, I placed my hands out and to my sides, and with an unguarded heart and at the top of my lungs, I called out, "Thank you Tucson, and thank you God for unknown blessings on their way! And so, it is."

I felt aligned here—even with all the fear of a loved one going through this health crisis, and I found that just one simple thank you would realign me, ground me, and create space for the good to find her and me.

As I meandered down the gravely steep hill, I paid extra close attention to the placement of each foot. I stopped to take in the beauty, and something caught my eye when I looked up at the magnificent clouds. Between two massive puffy clouds was a streaked image that looked identical to an angel. I walked the remainder of the way down, glancing back to see if she was still there. I snapped a picture because today's signs had officially overwhelmed me in the best of ways, and I wanted to capture one of them.

> "For He will command his angels concerning you to guard you in all your ways." Psalm 91:11 ESV

Not to my surprise, when I got to the bottom of the hill, the nurse called and was thrilled to tell me that they had repaired the aneurysm and everything should be smooth sailing from now on but that it would take an hour or so to finish.

"So, we aren't out of the woods by any means, but the trickiest parts are done," she explained.

I shared what I had just seen in the sky, and she sighed, "That's beautiful, Judy. I believe in angels, especially in this line of work. I was once blind, but now I see too." She giggled.

After the call, two hours passed, and I now wondered if there had been a complication.

I had arranged to be on our very first Zoom call with Lori Lane Dixon and all the women who were invited to write this book you have in your hands. Lori began with a group prayer, and so we all bowed our heads and prayed. Then my phone rang, and I quickly silenced it and moved away from the camera. I heard Lori's prayer in the background as I listened to the surgeon's voice. I was surprised to hear from him and immediately sat on a chair in case this was hard news. He then joyfully expressed that my mom did great and would soon be on her way to the recovery room!

With great relief, I gathered myself together and sat back in front of the camera. Lori had us introduce ourselves and share something about us and our work. I scribbled quick notes, knowing this would be hard while immersed in this massive relief.

When it came to me, I took a deep breath and then another. Then, instead of sharing about myself, I shared my open heart: "Ladies, the divine timing of meeting all of you today and Lori sharing our first prayer with a powerful intention for this book while having to step aside to take a surgeon's call, telling me that my mom's open-heart surgery was complete and successful, is proof that we don't walk alone. It's an honor to start this project with such divine timing. What a way to kick it off!"

> "We are all broken... that's how the light gets in."
> —Hemingway

I have found adversity to be grace in disguise. Everything that happens in our lives, whether it's a breakup, a diagnosis, a problematic turn of life events, the loss of a loved one, or any unforeseen circumstance, can leave our hearts cracked wide open. However, cracks have the potential to allow God to shine the light inside, which makes way for the blessings to come. And the cracks that heal are always stronger in the broken places. So, when I say adversity can serve you right, I mean that in the most divine way.

Sure, there are some things we have a role in and responsibility for manifesting in our lives, but the truth is that when we trust ourselves and God, we can create miracles together. One is to love on each other, see each other through good and hard times, and learn to live more consistently with an open heart so God can keep pouring his light in.

> "Learn to live more consistently with an open heart so God can keep pouring his light in."
>
> *judy cochrane*

In times filled with more ease and grace, when faced with this same open heart, the appreciation, and gratitude for the life you are living will only attract more goodness to you and yours.

Another thing I was able to take away while enduring this time was the ability to ask myself: Did I love others in my life with an open heart? And was I loving myself enough?

All in all, life is short. Don't waste time thinking you are here alone, carrying all the burden in times of crisis. Our supreme superpower gift is the ability to give love and receive love. With an open heart, you are more able to see the signs from above that remind us of where we come from—and that we are never alone. Signs give us proof of connection; they clarify that we are spiritual beings first, having this human experience second, and that we are walking alongside God. When we stay aware of our beliefs and clean them up when necessary, we can enjoy the ride where we can do, be, create, and heal anything, as it is all possible with God.

Keep the faith as you allow your open heart to guide you and align you with our trustworthy source, no matter what you face today or tomorrow. He's got you. In all ways. Always.

> "Above all else, guard your heart, for everything you do flows from it." Proverbs 4:23 NIV

Update on my mom: She had many magnificent synchronistic moments as she grew close to every nurse who cared for her. The surgeon released her from the ICU after only four days, and she has steadily recovered. All is well.

Prayer to God

Thank you.

"If the only prayer you ever say in your entire life is thank you, it will be enough." Meister Eckhart

Reflection

guard your heart, for everything you do flows from it

Proverbs 4:23

balance and bliss

Lori L. Dixon, Ed.S.

"Let joy (bliss) be your continual feast. Make your life a prayer. And always give thanks in everything, for this is God's perfect plan for you in Christ Jesus." 1 Thessalonians 5:17 The Passion Translation

Balance and bliss are two words that mean great things in our lives.

Where did my experience and knowledge about living in B&B come from? God's lessons as I was led into unique experiences in my life.

It all started with understanding balance first.

As an administrator of a therapeutic school partnered with my university, creating schedules for others required learning about schedules for myself. On one such significant learning experience, I can vividly remember the harsh reality and lesson I was meant to use to shift my perspective on BALANCE.

Pushing 80 hours a week working, I started crashing physically, mentally, emotionally, and spiritually. I remember one frightening day after long days, a week of grueling deadlines for paperwork and reports, and evening events where I had to be my "shining...full ON" self for everyone in attendance. That night I was more than exhausted. You know the feeling where your words don't come, your vision blurs, your body exhibits signs of shutting down, and all you want is a soft bed and sleep for about a week. My secretary would always know. I think she had radar or a tracking system on me for sure. She always knew when to say, "Lori, you need a hotel tonight, and I'm setting it up now." She would call a local hotel we agreed with for me and others when they were in town to do work for us. The hotel was less than five minutes away, and I could not drive that evening. Once I slowed down just enough, that was it. Then, the intense onset of a massive migraine began. My secretary, Dale, packed me up and took me to the hotel entrance. She lifted me out of the car and said, "I am marking you off for tomorrow, at least for the morning. I will call and check on you around noon." I nodded and pulled out my briefcase and travel bag (always packed for times like this). I can still see myself walking in the doors and to the front desk, as the manager, whom I knew well, took one look at me and said, "Oh, no, let's get you to your room! It is already set up for you." Bless his heart, and I know he was taken care of well by the university, and of course, Dale made sure he was, too.

Do I remember getting to my room that night? No. Do I even recall getting in my pajamas or even into bed? No. All I do remember was the knocking on my door the next day in the afternoon around 1:00 pm. I awoke from what felt like a dream of cloudiness to open the door to the front desk person handing me a bowl of chicken soup and a Coke (for my migraine). I could barely speak. I motioned thank you. He nodded and said, "You're welcome. Ms. Dale dropped these off for you. She wanted you to be checked on since it is afternoon, and she's been calling you." Could I have slept past noon and now into the afternoon? Dale knew. She made sure everything was taken care of, and I was asleep. I called the front desk and asked for an additional night, which had already been set up. As I crawled back into bed, I allowed myself to fall back asleep with nothing on my mind but a prayer of thankfulness for a beautiful team.

Was this the wake-up call I needed to create a new working method? I want to tell you yes, but there were more nights that year of my life with exhaustion, migraines, and even staying up all night working in my office. I eventually realized I couldn't sustain this pace. That is when the strangest things began happening, which led me to a change.

One day at work, I was running down the hall to a therapeutic classroom to assist a child. I reached out for the doorknob and fell into the door. What? I had reached to grab the round doorknob firmly and couldn't navigate my eye-hand coordination to function effectively. I fell directly into the door with my body because I had missed the "target" I was aiming for and physically couldn't react appropriately. I sat on the floor and called for Dale on the walkie-talkie back in the office, and she came over quickly. I knew I was in trouble. She called another administrator to help with the student, and we walked back slowly to the office.

"Lori…has this happened before?" she carefully probed. I responded with a firm and yes, freaked out, "NO!" We both decided I should call my doctor and see if they could get me in to have things looked at. Remember that I haven't mentioned I was also a doctoral student at the time and doing several rounds of courses in medical school, one of which was my passion, Neuroscience. I quickly reviewed what I knew about the brain and what could be happening and compiled a list of possible concerns. Not a good exercise and not one I would do with my clients right now. Thank goodness my doctors responded quickly, and I was scheduled for an MRI and more.

After all the tests were done, can you imagine what the outcome was for me? STRESS! My brain had created severe inflammation, and because the migraines were happening, the blood flow was constricted. What was the treatment? Guess again? My doctors prescribed yoga, meditation, fewer hours of uptime, better sleep habits, good health decisions, etc. We could control most of the migraines, and the inflammation also decreased. I began yoga many evenings a week near work and stopped working ALL weekend. Walking on the beach, being with friends and my sweetie, spending time with my dog, and not just bringing him to work with me and finding a NEW BALANCE within me.

I found time to go back to church, and my prayer time increased significantly, which I benefited greatly. So did all the people I was praying for, too. Let me share the rest of the story.

It all started with a pastor friend during my "running crazy 80 hours week cycle", who asked, "What are you doing this week?" I began listing out

"Even when we LOVE what we do, and it is our mission and purpose, God wants us to rest, too."

Lori L. Dixon

all the "have-to's" of life, the where's, and the "when's" of each scheduled task and appointment. His face showed his feelings and thoughts of what he was thinking then. So imagine his next question for me: "When do you rest and renew in the Lord?" Wow! I didn't prepare myself for that moment. As I took a deep breath, ready to launch into all of the "God needs me to work on His behalf with ..." Before I could even utter the first word, I couldn't believe what he said next, "Lori, you do know that Psalm 23 shares, that we will walk with the Lord, follow the Lord, accept his assignments in your life, strive to bring forth the kingdom of God on earth, AND... in between everything you are to LIE DOWN in GREEN PASTURES, too." I was drawn back and became quiet for a few minutes. I couldn't believe how God had just used someone in my life to give me the most remarkable example of the balance God asks for and demands in our life. Wow! He knows when we are called to do his mission, we get over-excited and run too fast, overlooking signs in the process and even ignoring that the purpose HE gave you requires...YOU! If YOU can't fulfill your assignment, it is at risk of being given to someone else or possibly not completed. Wow, again!

What did I do to change my schedule, my daily routine, my responsibilities, and my personal life? I invited God into every bit of it. With those two happenings, I succumbed to God's direction and returned to my personalized and unique mission. Over the years, many individuals have asked me if I truly believe that balance and bliss can exist in our life. I answered, "Of course...if it is done correctly." Yet, what is correct?

Here are a few of my strategies to support your possible insights as YOU shift:

1. **Use a planner (I use paper/marker type) of what flow I need daily throughout the week.** I still do this now, every Sunday afternoon. Monday is a push day for the week, laying out what needs to occur and checklists.... Tuesday is a client day, and I have learned to adjust the weekly hours depending on my load. Wednesday is a special day I will share with you next. I don't work on Wednesdays, yet I still do classes for myself in the evening. Thursday is a client day, sometimes women's business events. Good day to balance being OUT and being IN the office. Fridays are a catch-up day with clients, writing, and other things needed for the following week. I believe in the EBB and FLOW of my life. Saturdays are for events or family. Sundays are time with God and preparation for the week. Do I still have my device calendar with "scheduled times"? Yes, but the planner helps me create flow and almost journals my day for me to see patterns and ideas later.

2. **Focus on one week at a time. Place hours of existing appointments like doctors, clients, events, or responsibilities I may have into each of the days.** This may include exercise or mind break times, too. Then, I can start planning around them my "energy needed" or how I stay in "flow," things I may need to prepare, or lists I may need to make.

3. **Put in bible reading and prayer time every morning first thing.** Then, these don't get interrupted. I spend time in my weekly bible study and bible courses in which I am enrolled. Those are things that only get changed if there is an emergency.

4. **Buffer every appointment or event with a cushion.** I use 30 minutes on light days and an hour on heavy client days. If I only do 15-20 minutes with back-to-backs, I burn out by 4:00 pm, if not earlier. Your mind must download what your conversations were, follow-ups if needed, and even release time for that experience into a transition to the next.

5. For a long while, I taught programs in energy management for leaders to use with their staff. **As I have shared above, energy ebbs and flows throughout the day within each perceived and actual experience.** Scheduling high-energy moments with lower energy builds our capacity for better concentration, focus, engagement, and retention. Overall health depends on managing our energy output and our energy recuperation. I view each activity in my day as a "unit" of energy. When my output is too high, my immune system decreases, and so does yours. Your adrenals can't rebound if they don't have a way to monitor and manage their being ON and being OFF times.

6. **Color code times of having quiet, no stimulation, or pure peace, even for 15 minutes.** You choose your action and even have that change for you, too. Variety stimulates the brain in positive ways! This can be a bath, a quiet walk, sitting outside, breathwork, or anything you crave.

7. **Finally, every hour…move!** Take 3-5 minutes of standing, walking around, or breath work because your body must have frequent stops and starts to download information and to work optimally. When working from home, I do laundry, put away a few dishes, walk to the mailbox and back, stand up, and talk with a client. Your body will thank you.

8. Dedicate daily to God and find a way to live it out truthfully.

I have been sharing a lot about my balance journey, but when did the "B & B" begin? Learning about balance will be a lifelong journey for all of us. Due to my health being challenging, balance is crucial. Pacing myself allows me to see the goodness in my healing that God continues to bring. Whenever a health crisis occurs, I learn a little more. Such is the time for me to put the BLISS with my ongoing growth in BALANCE. It happened when we were excitedly awaiting the first grandson to be born.

I had been struggling with healing from back surgery, and the rehabilitation was intense. Unfortunately, it wasn't just my back; my right leg lacked functionality due to a damaged nerve. Being in a wheelchair for outings and using a cane at home was a reality. No matter how hard and fast I worked, the harsh reality was I might not have full function of the leg back. However, God told me differently. He and I had discussed it extensively, and I knew I would completely heal.

During one office visit with my surgeon, whom I dearly loved, he shook his head after I asked about my progress or lack thereof. Not knowing what to tell me, besides maybe placing a nerve stimulator into my back and wearing the pack on my side, I reluctantly and loudly said, "NO!" I began crying, and he just let me. Finally, he asked me, "What do you want to be able to do in your life? Can you tell me an action you want to do?" I thought momentarily and whispered, "I want to walk the stroller of my new grandchild on the way down to the neighbor's house." He smiled and said, "We can work with that." It became a goal toward BLISS. It made me realize how important my physical, mental, emotional, and spiritual BALANCE all works together for proper balance actions in our life.

What happened? God and my outstanding therapists worked with me as I kept the image of me walking down the street with the stroller in my head. Do I still have days of pain and weakness? Sometimes, God and I keep me going and He places new visions in my head to keep me focused and flowing. Was bliss a part of my healing? Of course, and it still is.

Did I know what BLISS was in my life? I thought I did. The minute my little grandson was placed into my arms for the first time, I saw, felt, heard, and even smelled true bliss. Having the sweetest granddaughters to spend time with in our lives was utterly fantastic. Still, we came into these opportunities a little later and cared for them short term times with one from a distance and during the summers, and the other beginning at six years old with after school, weekends, and of course, the summer. It was different. We craved to be an integral part of those beginning moments, holding them, rocking, feeding, and watching them grow.

What balance and bliss mean…

Balance is finding the flow of life amidst the overflowing and sometimes overwhelming life we lead. It is releasing what doesn't matter and receiving the goodness that God wants us to have in our life. It is the shift of mindset to realizing balance IS attainable when we let go and let God as we walk forward in each day with purpose and passion, not a schedule and a task list. When we plan out what you are "honoring" most in your day and week, God blesses it for you to carry out further His mission in YOU.

Bliss is the inner joy for us that we carry, knowing that God is our navigator and walking every day with us, every ebb and flow, every stroller walk, every quiet moment, and every car ride to work or to pick up our cherished children from school. That is bliss. It grows each time we create balance and recognize what matters in life. It is not chasing happiness and not looking for the next greatest job, relationship, "toy", increased influence or status, or even more money. The world's standards can't measure bliss but only by God's promises, wisdom, and direction in life for us. HIS overflowing presence and the Holy Spirit's presence in each moment bring true BLISS...bliss you can sensorily experience deep within your very spirit. It knows what matters and what to follow to keep this feeling—knowing that God is a consistent flow of perfect joy, love, compassion, direction, balance, and bliss for our life and a model for each to remember.

Each week I honor the balance and bliss God gives me. As I shared earlier in my strategy insights, I don't work Wednesdays. Guess why now? For eight years, Wednesdays have been called my "Balance and Bliss" days. My colleagues, friends, and clients know I don't work that day. I spent it with my two grandsons doing amazing things, hearing fabulous stories, and playing exciting games. Why? To remind them that we can have balance in our lives and that bliss is just as important in obtaining the best-balanced life. Are there moments I falter? Of course, the reminders of those times of being totally out of balance and not in bliss come crashing back in on me. It is the Holy Spirit's way of comforting us with peace and bliss and continuing the journey ahead. I know my grands are aware of when their Nana isn't. You will find me lying on the floor with them, watching a movie with rubbing backs, feet, and heads, reminding me to breathe. Doesn't that paint the best picture? Now find YOURS.

> "There is a time for everything and a season for every activity under the heavens." Ecclesiastes 3:1

"Now may God, the fountain of hope, fill you to overflowing with uncontainable joy and perfect peace as you trust in him. And may the power of the Holy Spirit continually surround your life with his super-abundance until you radiate with hope."
Romans 15:13 TPT

AMEN!

Reflection

make your life a prayer

1 Thessalonians 5:17

the walk of the warrior spirit

Deanna Blair

Realization: November 25th, 2018

As I scroll through my life over the last 18 years, I realize the pieces of my puzzle are finally starting to fit.

The dots are finally connecting.

People I've met, the places I've gone... one by one, it's slowly coming along.

The decisions I've made... good and bad, are not always easy, but... they turned out pretty rad.

Sometimes that one wrong decision we fought off years ago...we thought we'd never hear the end of it or ever let it go.

But, it turns out that one wrong decision is a storybook untold.

So, as I continue this journey through life, I look forward to seeing this unfinished tale unfold.

Every day has a purpose, so find yours.

> "And we know that in all things God works for the good of those who love him, who have been called according to his purpose." Romans 8:28

My spiritual journey started in 2013 when I was in a tumultuous relationship. I had accepted Jesus as my Lord and Savior when I was nine, but I hadn't prayed in many years... or at least with much depth, let alone repented for the thousands of sins I committed. My already less-than-pea-size faith was dwindling by the day. Ultimately, I knew God forgave me, but I yearned to be close to Him.

As I learned to be honest with myself and understand the gravity of an affair in my eight-year marriage resulting from a horrible relationship, I realized I was living my worst nightmare. This wasn't short-term either. He and I saw each other for over six months before I moved out of my marital house and into his.

My marriage was losing its magic... or that's what I thought. I felt like we had lost our communication with each other. Whenever I wanted to talk, he was too busy with work or so tired from his long day that he didn't want to spend time with me until the next morning. Well, morning would come, and we would still never have the time to discuss US and what WE needed to do to save our marriage. When he was ready to talk, I hung out with friends at my favorite local bar or restaurant because I was "letting traffic die down." That's what I told myself, oh, and my husband. This routine became a regular habit for me, along with talking to every guy at the bar who wanted to converse with me. They fulfilled the craving within me for interaction, connection, and, yes, attention. The more time I "waited for the traffic to die down," the more dinners I had by myself. The later nights with my hubby working all the time, he had more dinners by himself. It was a continuous cycle for both of us.

Then… I met Greg[†], the "other" guy, at a well-known charity event I attended every month. It so happened I was there volunteering when I walked up on this handsome man standing next to the bar. We started talking. The very thing I WASN'T doing with my husband. The conversations with Greg flowed fluently like we had known each other for years. By the end of the night, we were friends on Facebook. I didn't think much about it. I wasn't looking for anything from him. It was "just" a conversation… or so I thought.

There were many things that I should have questioned before moving forward with him. For example, I changed my profile picture one day because I got tired of having the same one and wanted something new. Several people commented on how great I looked in the picture. I didn't think much of it but was grateful for the kind words. But Greg had different words for me. He said, "Wow, you like that attention, don't you? Did you really need to change your picture so you could get all that attention?" I noted what he said and wrote it off as interesting, yet not my intention! I told him that wasn't the reason for the picture change, but he still had opinions. I brushed it aside, but I should have looked at this interaction

---

*[†] I changed his name for confidentiality purposes.

as a red flag as it was a small peek at his narcissistic behavior waiting to rear its ugly head.

Six months later, as we began seeing each other more often and, of course, me lying my way through the affair with my husband, Greg issued an ultimatum. He started by saying he wanted to see me more often and turned down women to be with me. He wanted me for himself and would no longer share me with my husband. He wanted me to move in with him and leave my husband.

Realization: I now look at that and understand his power over me. The manipulation was beginning.

I didn't want to leave my husband, but I didn't want to end things with Greg. I didn't know what to do. Greg kept telling me he had opportunities to go places with this other woman and would probably start seeing her more often. I didn't want that. I wanted to be with him and didn't want anyone else to take my place. How could I have felt this way?

Realization: It was my worth I was struggling with, and I couldn't see it.

Greg pressured me to move in with him in the coming days. I was struggling with my marriage; I was struggling with keeping my business open. Everything was sinking because I had lost interest in building what my husband and I had created. I wanted a simpler life. I kept thinking that the life I could have with Greg would be simple. I wouldn't have to worry about anything but making him happy. I just KNEW the grass would be greener on the other side… was I ever wrong!

A week later, I found myself packing up boxes in my home. Was I leaving everything I had built, along with my business, cat, and husband, to be with someone I only knew briefly? What a disaster! From day one, yes, the day I moved in with him, I knew it was the wrong relationship. I knew I had just made the biggest mistake of my life. I was heartbroken at what I had just done to my husband and my life. I couldn't get my head on straight to save my life. I was depressed beyond measure.

Greg aggressively told me, "You should be happy. We are together now." I wasn't happy at all! What I had just done was crushing me, but I thought I couldn't go back. The damage was done. A week went by, and all we did was fight. Greg hated my life before him. He hated the physical and emotional things I brought to his house.

Realization: The manipulation was shifting to abuse. In my heart, I could feel it. Yet, my mind wouldn't let me change my circumstance.

Greg never trusted me and was paranoid, mentally abusive, and controlling. He said that for him to trust me, I had to give him passwords to every application in my world. I reluctantly gave in to this unreasonable demand. After I fell asleep, he would go through old emails that I hadn't seen or thought about in years. He covered it up by saying he once worked with the CIA and still had connections to get people's information. He would also go through my LinkedIn and Facebook pages and message colleagues to let them know that I was married and to never talk to me again. I didn't find out until I was out of the relationship. I even terminated my Facebook account, trying to stop his verbal abuse.

He accused me of lying, saying I never told him about one situation or the next. At first, I still needed to learn where he got his information. The things he would accuse me of not telling him always happened many years before we met. Some of the things he accused me of lying about were so mind-blowing that I had to seriously dig deep to recall them. He went so far as to make up complete lies. I had known this man for less than six months, and he asked me to remember details from insignificant moments from years past.

It was draining. Every day I would wake up wondering what was going to happen next. What kind of drama was in store for the day? He told me several times that I would never amount to anything outside him… I showed him later down the road that he was wrong.

Life with this man became my nightmare. Week after week, he either accused me of something or thought I was seeing someone behind his back. That was interesting since he basically grounded me to the house. I had to ask permission to go to the grocery store or down the street to work out. I was scared for the first time that I wouldn't get out of this situation any time soon. Greg told me to remove people from my life. He tried pushing me away from my dad by telling me we talked too often.

I realized the "relationship" would never improve from the beginning, and I began praying. I prayed long and hard daily for the Lord to rescue me from this tyrant. I had no idea what to pray for other than, "Please make this stop. Please help me get out of this horrible situation." I clung to God and prayed without ceasing. I knew He was listening to me when I couldn't speak to anyone else.

> "With God, all things are possible for those who believe." Matthew 19:26

> "Rejoice in hope, be patient in tribulation, be constant in prayer." Romans 12:12

As the relationship got worse, I got closer to God. The fighting was daily, lack of sleep and tons of stress. I lost a giant ball of hair that left a massive gap on my scalp that I had to cover with other pieces of my hair. The only place I was allowed to cry was in the bathroom, and I had to be extremely quiet. Sometimes I would get in my car, drive around for a few minutes, and sit in the grocery store parking lot, crying my eyes out. I couldn't let my feelings show because he insisted that I should be overwhelmed with joy. After all, we were together now.

> "Cast your burden on the Lord, and he will sustain you; he will never permit the righteous to be moved." Psalm 55:22

Realization: I was a victim, and I felt trapped. He was out of control, the textbook definition of a narcissist. The abuse was intense, yet in those moments, leaving was not an option... or so I thought. I was determined not to live as a victim.

Weeks passed, and there was finally peace in the house without constant fighting. Because I told him in the beginning that I missed my cat dearly, instead of sharing that I missed my old life, he took me to an animal shelter. I didn't want to be there with him. I was angry and hated him for everything. I found two brother and sister kittens that clung to me like I was their mother. I was torn. I wanted MY cat back. I wanted MY life back. I put the male down, and he immediately got swooped up by a little girl who adored him. She asked me if I wanted him, and with big tears in my eyes, I said no. The kitten and I held onto one another for dear life. The longer I stood there, the less I wanted to leave her, so she came home with us.

I can't begin to tell you how this tiny little kitten changed my world. She was everything I needed from that moment through the next several months. She knew when I was sad, which was most of the time. She was always on or near me and was a very affectionate little human-like kitty. I loved her and was so thankful she was in my life. She kept me going when I felt like I couldn't any longer.

As months passed, at least we were not fighting as much. I had been there a year and had become numb because I had missed my life more than ever. I spoke with my ex-husband a few times. We shared small talk, and I realized how much I missed him. But, in the end, there would always be this significant predicament if we were ever to get back together. He had a lot of hurt and distrust that he couldn't get past, and we both needed a lot of healing. I just wanted him back.

I finally worked up the courage to leave, and after making an elaborate plan that included my dad and a close friend, the time was near. Not sure of the exact date, but it gave me hope that an end to this nightmare was coming. Grateful to God for the strength to have endured this for a year, I excitedly looked forward to my future.

I had been working upstairs for several hours, organizing music from several collections into one file. Then, unexpectedly, an enraged Greg stormed upstairs with fire coming out of his nose. He was furious!

He yelled, "You can go ahead and take that job you just applied for on LinkedIn!"

I looked at him, puzzled. "I have no idea what you are talking about. I've been working on organizing music for the last few hours."

It turned into a heated yelling match of him, once again, accusing me of lying when I wasn't even near LinkedIn. He said, "I was on your LinkedIn account, and it says you just looked up a job."

I said, "I haven't looked at LinkedIn in weeks."

He grabbed my phone and ran downstairs with me chasing him. The yelling match continued as he told me to leave his house. He stormed off, grabbing my clothes, throwing them into my car, and screaming at me the entire time. Gathering most of my belongings, I prayed quietly, "Thank you, Lord, for this huge opportunity for him to actually invite me to leave." I felt so much peace.

Realization: I look back now and firmly believe that God opened the door for me to walk through. What a horrific and traumatic year that I could finally leave behind!

That night, I stayed with my friend, who lived a few minutes away from Greg's house. It was nice to sleep in peace that night, but I was anxious to see him the next day when I returned for my cat and a handful of things left behind.

I called the police the next day for an escort to and into his house. To my surprise, several cop cars pulled up just as I arrived. WOW, now that's God! I found out later that the police were no strangers to his house. No surprise.

Four officers stayed in the living room with him, while one stayed with me as I gathered my belongings. Walking through the rooms, I realized that Greg had hidden or trashed many of my things, some gone forever. As I picked up my cat to leave, he was adamant that she belonged to him and that I couldn't take her. As we both got heated, the police said we would have to work out those details later. I was heartbroken to leave her.

I drove off with tears covering my face… happy that I was free, sad because I needed my cat, and uncertain as to where my life was going from this point forward. But that moment was the first time I felt I could breathe in over a year.

While there were times when Greg displayed compassion and care, he usually revealed extreme narcissistic behavior. Now with him in my rearview mirror, I had time to think, reflect, and pray. I wondered what I saw in him. Why didn't I spot the warning signs? I was enticed, physically and emotionally, by him. What caused me to be lured into that type of behavior? I know now that Narcissists cling to people with self-esteem problems, such as those who have experienced abuse or trauma. Having grown up with my mom, who has suffered from severe mental illness since I was a young child, I could write a book about trauma and mistreatment. My mom was diagnosed with paranoid schizophrenia when I was nine. My parents divorced when I was around ten because of her illness. My dad always wanted his marriage to work out with my mom, but she demanded a divorce. She always thought my dad, as well as everyone else, was out to get her. That's a primary symptom of schizophrenia. Always thinking people want to harm you or paranoid that someone is stalking you, or thinking someone is following you 24/7. My mom even thought people lived in our attic for a while, which was even scarier when you're nine years old and unsure what's happening.

The challenges I went through with my mom being diagnosed with paranoid schizophrenia helped me understand and deal with the paranoia I went through with Greg... only it was on a different scale. I could keep my composure with Greg during most situations, whereas with my mom, I always blew up and didn't have the right words to say.

Her mental illness left a massive burden on my family for years. I lived with my dad for many years growing up. What I realized from being apart from my mom was that I lacked the nurturing side of me that I didn't know until I went through the relationship with Greg.

To this day, even though I couldn't stand him, Greg helped me build the pieces of me back together to become a better person than I am today. There is more of my mom's story coming soon! Stay tuned.

Realizations from my "walk": I have gained wisdom along the way. Am I completely healed? I am a work in progress. The deep emotional wounds brought on by this man will take a while to unravel. Yet, I now understand my worth in Christ and can lean into my past as I continue to walk with the true one who loves me as God continues to deliver me through the hardships in life.

As I write this part of my story, I reflect on the years it has taken to get from one point to another. Even though I've had a lot of challenges after leaving this toxic relationship, it's been the best thing I could have ever done, and I wouldn't change a thing. So, I accept I am a "work in progress" and blessed beyond imagination!

> "My children, listen to what your father teaches you. Pay attention, and you will have wisdom." Proverbs 4:1

My cat, Bella, whom I left behind with Greg, was the joy I hadn't had in my relationship for that year. I missed the joys in my life throughout that time while thinking about my ex-husband and my other cat. After I left Greg, there were countless things that I realized he had stolen from me. Clothing, shoes, anything that was of value to me was gone. All I kept thinking about was how I missed Bella dearly and created this life because of an affair.

As time passed, I prayed to God that Greg was caring for Bella. I didn't bring her with me because my new roommate had two dogs, and she had already mentioned that I couldn't bring her. I was aggravated with my roommate about that situation. Bella was my family, but neither wanted me to take her.

As years passed, I realized why Bella wasn't in my life. I moved many

"I accept I am a 'work in progress' and blessed beyond imagination!"

deanna blair

times to various places where God showed me that it would have been challenging to have her with me everywhere I moved, and I might have lost her throughout that time. Throughout the moves in my life, God also helped me gain more wisdom about who he truly wanted me to become through various situations. He wanted me to cling to him and not anyone or anything else. After four long brutal years, the Lord finally allowed me to have another kitten that I named Grace. She's been with me ever since. Even though I had multiple challenges, she has been a little breath of fresh air. She reminds me of a cat I lost years ago when I briefly lived with my mom. That's God's grace… giving back to me a hundredfold.

> "Anyone who does the will of my Father in heaven, is my brother, and my sister, and mother." Matthew 12:50

Prayer to God

Thank you, Father, for bringing me out of the slimy pit I once lived through. It would have been far more difficult without you by my side. You have been instrumental throughout my whole journey. As I continue to run the race with perseverance, the race laid out for me, I can't wait to see what lies in this next season.

In your mighty name, I pray, Amen!

I pray for the women this may resonate with at this moment. YOU are worthy. Your life has a great purpose and calling. Never let go of your freedom and choice so you may reach the "mile markers" laid out just for you. We are with you, dear sister!

Amen and Amen!

Amen means "and so it is"! Don't you feel it?!

If you or anyone you know is experiencing a relationship with narcissism, control, or abuse, please call the National Domestic Violence Hotline for help at 1-800-799-7233.

Your life has worth in the eyes of the Lord! You are His child, and He is here for you! We pray for this stronghold over your life and know God will release you from pain and bring you toward freedom.

Reflection

pay attention, and you will have wisdom

Proverbs 4:1

walk of growth

She Was Shamelessly Courageous

Stephanie Vasquez

"She wraps herself in strength, might, and power in all her works. She tastes and experiences a better substance, and her shining light will not be extinguished, no matter how dark the night is." Proverbs 31:17-19

She was mouthy, crass, promiscuous, an addict, and incredibly aggressive. She was hurt from the years of neglect and lacked identity from never feeling heard or loved. She looked for her worth in others and was always undervalued.

As I write this story, if it weren't for the emotional remembrances that came with it, I wouldn't even recognize the woman I was then. To have met me years ago, you would be as surprised as I am at the woman God has led me to become.

Witnessing what God was able to see within someone so broken from her perception, to create a new person who is shamelessly persistent in seeking Him, and see her evolve from worthless to worth-filled. What I love most is her shamelessly relentless spirit and how she loves God!

I am blessed to be that woman... yes, both of them! The overflowing understanding of how God can and will make your spirit "anew" in Him has been my journey. How did this whole transformative experience begin? Let me share my story with you.

I met God, or should I say, God met me at the beginning of a horrendously terrible marriage. I grew up in a broken home with no father figure. It was just my mother, who is still dealing with many of her scars and wounds in life. As one can imagine, I had no idea what a good marriage was, what a good husband looked like, nor how to be a good wife. Yet, I jumped in any way with both feet, dismissing every. Single. Red flag and said, "I do." And I did this based on what I thought was a green light from the Lord. Unfortunately, my awareness of hearing His voice and truly listening wasn't yet a reality. Now that I understand the meaning of discernment, I would hear Him say, "This is a hard NO." Fortunately, my new awareness is grounded in serving a God of grace, which abounds.

I grew up in church and memorized Psalm 23 and the "Our Father" prayer like every other church-going Christian. But what did that even mean? Who was God? What was His part in my life anyway? I knew God was always with me. Yet, even at my darkest moments, I heard a tiny whisper that said, "This is not for you," or "You need to leave right now." Yet, I didn't realize that it must've been important if I heard it clearly and wasn't following Him!

As I prayed before walking down the hall at my Las Vegas wedding, I was sure everything would turn out fine. Was I in denial and didn't know it? So many couples get married with serious wounds to heal, and they do it together.

Things were already tumultuous as we left our elopement and mini honeymoon to the Grand Canyon. We arrived home to find out we were both now unemployed and getting evicted. I couldn't see that this was a sign from God to leave. We shouldn't be together. Instead, I took it as an obstacle from the enemy to see if we would last. With me being as stubborn as can be, we continued with our marriage.

As we put all our belongings into the U-Haul from our apartment, I heard the Holy Spirit say, "Don't worry, I have a plan. I'm right here with you." That was comforting. As the saying goes, things often get worse before they get better. We fought all the time. He couldn't keep a job due to depression and alcoholism. I made excuses for his behavior until I turned to the one thing I knew I could count on, God. I may not have learned much about God then; we certainly didn't have a relationship, but I did know that He can change lives drastically.

I convinced my then-husband that we needed to start attending church, stop living frivolously, and get into Christian-led counseling. We came upon a mega church in Dallas that offered a group marriage counseling program, so we went. As we sat there listening to the testimonies of other couples and how bad their marriage had been, I thought to myself, surely that can be our story too. Whether we were getting better or it was just me, I was making it a point to seek God, read His word, and pray. I was intentional. I wanted the type of change that I heard so many others talk about. Like all the others, our marriage had many ups and downs, which I thought was normal.

As "we" drew closer to God, the pandemic happened. Like many families, we were in a tough place. We lived in a studio apartment with my two children above a relative's home. What a mess: two adults, two kids, one tiny space, plus the pandemic. It was the opposite of the ideal. A few months before, I started working in insurance and financial services. If you don't already know, this can be a brutal line of work, and the pandemic didn't make it any easier. My husband, who couldn't straighten his life, convinced me to have a baby. I was very reluctant as I was already a single mother with two children and did not want to go through it with three. He professed that he wouldn't leave; he'd get his act together and care for us. I realize now that I was so broken and desperate. What was I thinking?

Because of my complicated past, I had severe abandonment issues. These were evident by the choices I made and the broken promises I continued to believe. My family's challenges were profound. Therefore, as an adult, I wanted to please my husband, thinking that's what a good wife would do. I was hoping he would fill a void that had been empty for so many years. I realized much later that God alone could fill this emptiness, and nothing could complete me the way He did.

Of course, I did get pregnant, and for a short time, my husband and I were turning a corner. He was more attentive, sweeter, and looked and acted as if he was genuinely trying to be the husband we all needed. But, after the baby was born, he returned to his usual self. Then, finally, reality started sinking in that I was alone in my marriage and parenting.

I was also the only one working. I got a job selling Medicare Advantage plans over the phone, with a new baby next to me, while my husband would sleep off the alcohol from the night before. This wasn't working. As I struggled with postpartum depression, it triggered my abandonment issues all over again. Sitting on the couch with my baby boy and autodialer, I cried out to God. In that desperate moment, God nudged me to open a bible app I had for my phone. It was there for me with words of comfort and answers. I would read yet another scripture for each person who didn't answer the phone that night. It prompted me to sign up for a way to read the bible in a year  plan. If ever there was something to fill the void of not talking to anyone, this would be it, and instead…God showed up in each word I read.

But God wasn't done with me yet! Eventually, I got a much better-paying job, and we could move from our three-bedroom apartment into a rented house in a fantastic neighborhood way out of our price range. Walking with the Lord has become a daily experience now in my life. During this transition, I started to feel the pull of the Holy Spirit, asking me to journal and write down scriptures to be further open to Him. So, I eagerly did. It unleashed a hunger and a fire for God I never knew I could feel! The more I released myself to God, the more I learned about Him, His promises, and what He desired for me and my life. It even lessened how I reacted and engaged in everyday arguments with my husband. Instead, the Holy Spirit filled me with pure joy and contentment in the Lord, and my husband was jealous of it.

As my search for God's truth persisted, so did my husband's insecurities and outlandish behavior. I grew accustomed to our frequent arguments and disagreements, yet I was unphased. As much as I wanted to put the entire blame on him, I had my part in it too. I didn't have to stay. But I thought I was doing what God wanted me to, and He gave me lots of grace and taught me how to be a supportive, understanding wife.

God grew me a lot in that season. I became more compassionate as I realized how much compassion God had for me. I was a sinner, living in sin, and my actions warranted death, and yet He forgives, grants grace, and continues walking right next to us. He allows us to live more abundantly in Him or try doing life on our own. Understanding God's love for me, and the sacrifice He made, makes everything else seem so small. Eventually, God called me to leave my

"I became more compassionate as I realized how much compassion God had for me."

stephanie vasquez

great-paying job and work strictly on commission. It was a massive leap of faith; I must've asked for every sign. When I finally obeyed, God made a plan to make it work.

Sometimes, God asks us to do uncomfortable things, take a leap of faith, and trust Him. When I did this, things worked out for my good. As Romans 8:28 says:

> And we know that all things work together for good to them that love God, to them who are the called according to his purpose.

As things further deteriorated with my marriage, God was kind enough to send some fantastic God-filled people into my life. God protected me with people who genuinely cared, prayed for me, and with me as I battled demons from my past and in my own home. He protected me.

One day, our son got sick, and later that night, I got sick, which rarely happens. I looked at the clock. 4 am and my husband was missing. I was infuriated, to say the least, especially when I called him to find out he was "hanging out" at someone else's house. He was so unremorseful about it; I finally saw even if I didn't value myself, I, without a doubt, knew I deserved better. I talked to a great spiritual mentor, and she said, "Yes, it's time for you to leave. God has given you a door, and it's time to leave it."

As we are all God's children, it is never His intent for any of His children to be mistreated or abused, whether physically, mentally, or emotionally. God wants the best for us. All of us. He does not like for anyone to do otherwise. When I finally left, my husband asked me why. I said, "God sees my heart and yours too." He didn't have anything to say.

The season that came after, although it was a relief to leave, came with much heartache. I found out so many lies about my husband. God saw it all. He knew it all. He gave my husband a chance to be a father and a husband.

> "Call me, and I will answer you and tell you great and unsearchable things you do not know." Jeremiah 33:3

Humans tend to ask God "why" when life happens around us. Why did this happen to me? Why did you let me do this? The answer is because He loves you, and you have free will over your life. We ask "why," but we weren't looking for God while living recklessly. I assure you, though, He was always looking for us. He is right there with us in every step we take. God wants the best for us, and now I believe I have made that the standard for myself, my children, and anyone else God may choose to let into our lives.

As I sit here writing this to you now, I have come to a place where I have found joy in being a single parent of three. God has allowed me to see how He sees me; a sinner made perfect by the blood of Jesus Christ. While I still have moments like Haggar did in the wilderness, in a predicament that is not exactly where I belong, I am exactly where God wants me to be. As Haggar said, we serve a God who SEES us. He meets us exactly where we are, and no matter how much pain, brokenness, and mess there is, He still wants a relationship with us. He wants nothing more than for us to go to Him for everything. The scripture says he delights in the details of our lives. There is nothing too big or small to kneel and go to our Father.

This is from Paul's letter to the people of Corinth and the many churches throughout southern Greece. We are indeed brothers and sisters in the Lord.

> "If troubles weigh us down, that means we will receive even more comfort to pass on to you for your deliverance! For the comfort pouring into us empowers us to bring comfort to you. And with this comfort upholding you, you can endure victoriously the same suffering that we experience. Our hope for you is unshakable because we know that just as you share in our sufferings, you will also share in God's comforting strength." 2 Corinthians 1:6-7

Prayer to God

Dear Lord: I pray for the person my story resonates with at this moment, wherever they are in their own journey. I pray for their heart and their sorrow. I pray that this has given them a glimpse of hope to see that they are never alone. May they be able to stand in courage to make the hard decisions, look at themselves in the mirror, and see themselves the way You see them, Father. You see them as Your perfect creation, uniquely designed. I pray for their healing and a brighter tomorrow. I pray that you grant them the faith of a mustard seed to take the next necessary steps in their lives. Show them how much you love them, Lord, and that wherever they are right now is not the end of their story. You are the author and finisher of our faith, creator, and reason for joy. I thank you, Lord, for the opportunity to encourage them through my own story. Let them be blessed to experience the life of abundance you have promised us in your word. May we all learn to be "shamelessly persistent" in our prayers as we walk courageously and passionately for God. Amen.

Reflection

Call me, and I will answer you...

Jeremiah 33:3

you can't hug a palm tree

Lori L. Dixon, Ed.S.

> "The greatest legacy one can pass on to one's grandchildren is not money or other material things accumulated in one's life, but rather a legacy of character and faith."
> —Billy Graham

My Mom loved to tell stories and read to me most of my life, even into adulthood. We both shared a passion for all kinds of books, especially children's literature. It is one of the reasons I have written books for kids and publish them now, too. Our children deserve wonderful stories with beautiful meanings and lessons paired with brilliant illustrations to capture their creativity.

My Mom, Loretta, always wanted to write a book for grandparents who were not close in a geographical area with their grandchildren. She is the one who started the book called "You Can't Hug a Palm Tree" because moving away from her only grandchild at the time was painful. Mom wanted him always to know how much she loved him. This story is for her, my precious Mom, lover of great food, entertaining children of all ages, jokes and humor, deep friendships, her faith in God, and BOOKS!

Want to hear the story? I can't wait to share my mom's creative ideas about how a grandma was sharing about the move that she and grandpa would be taking very soon.

"Why all the boxes?" the young grandson, Nathaniel, asked.

Grandma Loretta let Nathaniel peek inside one of the boxes being packed. "Inside each box is something special from our home that we want in our new home in Florida." Nathaniel thought momentarily and asked, "Will pictures of my family and I be in the boxes? Where will you put them in Florida?" Grandma told him how the bookcases in this house would accompany us to the new home and be placed in a new room. His pictures and photo albums would be on that same bookcase for Grandpa and Grandma to look at daily.

"What about my favorite toys I like to play with when I'm in this house? Where will they go?" Grandma explained they were going to Florida for him to come and play in the new yard, go to new parks, and take on long walks with her and Grandpa.

"Will we come to visit you a lot like we do now?" his curious mind was playing ahead.

"You will come and stay longer with us instead of the short visits we have now," she shared to appease him.

Grandma Loretta had to turn away momentarily to wipe a tear from her eye before her little guy would see it and become concerned.

Grandma and Nathaniel started backpacking the boxes and sealing them shut with names on them for the movers to take to Florida and unload there. Nathaniel asked what the words were on each one and how the new house would have different rooms and no stairs to climb. Instead, we will enjoy a new type of room screened in for sitting outside, watching the birds and the squirrels, called a "lanai." She gave him images to hold on to and know where things would be to reassure him of each step toward the change for both of them. Finally, she asked herself, "What am I going to do… you can't hug a palm tree!" Nathaniel crawled up on her lap and hugged her tightly, quietly whispering as he fell asleep from all the "work" they were doing, "I love you, Grandma. I will send you hugs in big boxes!"

It was moving truck day, and Grandma and Grandpa directed the movers to carefully load everything tight and snug for the long trip. Grandma thought about how Nathaniel had helped her pack some of the boxes and even put kisses and hugs for her to open when she got to Florida…where that was.

Nathaniel knew it was far away because his mommy had shared how Grandma and Grandpa would drive for almost three days to get there. The boxes would take a bit longer, so Nathaniel was worried about Grandma not having a hug to keep her "filled up" until the packages arrived. He decided to draw her hugs, color them with bright colors of blue and green (Grandma's favorites), and give them to them as they drove away. Grandma tucked her drawings in her purse and kept them safe. She prayed and asked God to bring her peace during this time.

"And the peace of God, which surpasses all understanding, will guard your hearts and your minds in Christ Jesus." Philippians 4:7

Once Grandma and Grandpa reached the new house and pulled into the new driveway, they smiled at each other. Their new home was a dream they had together all these years, and yes, there were palm trees in the front yard. They crawled out of the car, and Grandma Loretta brought her hand-drawn pictures out of her purse and put them on the new refrigerator so they were there when she needed a hug.

They explored their new city and even went to the beaches nearby, where they knew they would walk quite often. Grandpa turned to Grandma as they walked past one of the many palm trees by the beach. Grandma smiled a slight grin and hugged Grandpa tight. She whispered to God, "You still can't hug a palm tree."

Weeks and months went by, and palm trees would remind Grandma of the hugs her little grandson would give her, and the ones from the refrigerator were now in frames and hanging in the new house. Then, one particular day, her phone rang, and the voice on the other end said, "Grandma, how are my hugs to you? Did you get the ones out of the boxes, too?" Grandma answered with a laugh and happy tears as she shared how they made her feel and Grandpa, too. Then, the best words ever were shared, "Grandma? Mommy and I are coming to see you in Florida!"

Grandma screamed with delight and ran to find Grandpa on the lanai to share the good news. They couldn't believe it!

A visit from their extraordinary boy and their amazing daughter, too. The plans began on what they would do and how long they could stay. It would be a trip of many blessings.

As Grandma and Grandpa drove to the airport, seeing all the palm trees lining the way was a sign from God that real hugs were almost there. This was the way. Grandma giggled aloud and shared her thoughts with Grandpa, who smiled and said, "They are almost here." Pulling up to the airport and watching people coming out, they finally saw a little boy jumping up and down, arms stretched out, with a tall, red-haired daughter pushing a big baggage cart closer to the car. They all ran to meet each other, and Nathaniel hugged and hugged and hugged some more as he shared, "I've been saving them all up for YOU."

The drive home was filled with showing everything that made this new place, Florida, feel a little less far away. "Here's our favorite restaurant, there's the church we love, here's where we buy bagels, and…" Grandma and Grandpa pointed out and labeled for their visitors. Then, they were interrupted with, "Grandma, there are lots of palm trees…LOOK!" Grandma Loretta laughed and exclaimed, "But you can't HUG a palm tree. I needed YOU!"

This story was a dream for my mom, Loretta. She taught me to love and appreciate the importance of children's stories and how sometimes they bring more meaning and simplicity to life than all adult books. I can still see her sitting on the front porch of our house in Illinois as a child. She would only have to bring out a book and tell me it was story time, and I would come from anywhere I was playing to hear the rhythmic text, the sound of the words describing scenes, people, and occurrences in the characters' lives. All my friends in the neighborhood would come running to lay on the porch or the grass in the front yard, drink lemonade, and hear about places far away and strange adventures of mice who road motorcycles, chocolate factories with unbelievable happenings, and big giant peaches.

I read those stories to my grandchildren now and still hear my mom's voice as I do. Mom's story of "You Can't Hug a Palm Tree" was her request to become a book for all the grandparents who live away or can't see their grands to feel better and know they ARE loved.

> "It is our calling and mission from God to walk the path he places us on and to affect the people and places we encounter every day."
>
> *lori l. dixon*

As an administrator, I created a children's library and dedicated it to my mom. See, I believe deeply in our life's legacy. It is our calling and mission from God to walk the path he places us on and to affect the people and places we encounter every day. Unfortunately, the library didn't happen; God told me to name my publishing company LLD Legacy Publishing. Why? Lori Lane Dixon includes my maiden and family name. I was named after my mom, Loretta Lane, so it is a legacy to her through the life assignment on which God has placed me.

As for the children's story, I am sharing it with you today as a glimpse of what is coming in our next children's book for LLD Legacy Publishing. I know you will want to read it, and I pray YOU will.

Now on the following page, reflect and write YOUR legacies you are carrying. How will YOUR legacy be remembered? You will be glad you have them with you. I thank God for the legacies in your life and your family's life. Honor them, and dedicate them back to God. I know he has dramatically blessed you with GRACE gifts, too. Please share them with us. They ARE part of your legacy.

Reflection

the peace of God will guard your hearts and your minds

Philippians 4:7

the walk of what if to I wonder

My Story of Surrendering in Faith to Hear God's Voice

Becky Dozeman, MSW, LMSW

As I share my story with you, hear the invitation as He guides your steps. Read the below verses in two different Bible translations and focus on how different the words vary, but the message remains the same. Absorb these words and how they enhance your understanding of who God is in your life.

> "The LORD makes firm the steps of the one who delights in him; though he may stumble, he will not fall, for the LORD upholds him with his hand." Psalms 37: 23-24 NIV

> "When Yahweh delights in how you live your life, he establishes your every step. If they stumble badly, they will still survive, for the Lord lifts them up with his hands." Psalm 37:23-26 TPT

You may be saying to yourself this life is not what I imagined. But, fortunately, or unfortunately, the life you thought you'd have is not what you are experiencing.

Friend, you are living a normal and quite common reality.

By the way, I don't use "friend" lightly. Friendship is created through intimate, repeated connections of sharing stories, space, and community experiences. Although our paths may not have crossed, we are friends because we are sisters in Christ, which makes our worlds intersect. In Christ, our community is inherent.

Not many of us look back over our lives and think, "Yup, it all went as planned!" But, if you're a list-maker like me, you could write out what has yet to go as you expected. Throughout our lives, we'll inevitably experience periods of: How did I get here? What happened? Who am I? Is this the way it's supposed to be? How come it isn't going this way instead of that? Why are things going like that for her and this for me?

During these seasons of questioning, the Lord prunes us for HIS will. This pruning is part of the process. Yet, this pruning can only occur IF you spend sacred time in HIS presence!

I have struggled in various seasons with how to sit in the quiet space of HIS presence. I've also walked alongside clients and friends who have wrestled with carving out deep intimacy in Him. I clumsily stumbled along this journey for years. So many words come to mind to describe this experience of desiring closeness with the Lord but feeling something was missing. Something was not right. In reading and trying to put my proverbial finger on it, I finally found clarity and hope in the words of Henri Nouwen.

Solitude is the furnace of transformation. Without solitude, we remain victims of our society and continue to be entangled in the illusions of the false self. Jesus himself entered this furnace in the wilderness. There he was tempted with the three compulsions of the world: to be relevant ("turn stones into loaves"), to be spectacular ("throw yourself down"), and to be powerful ("I will give you all these kingdoms"). But instead, he affirmed God as the only source of his identity ("You must worship the LORD your God and serve him alone").

Solitude is the place of the great struggle and the great encounter—the struggle against the compulsions of the false self and the encounter with the loving God who offers himself as the substance of the new self.

> In solitude, I get rid of my scaffolding: no friends to talk with, no telephone calls to make, no meetings to attend, no music to entertain, no books to distract me, just me...The task is to persevere in my solitude and stay in my cell until all my seductive visitors get tired of pounding on my door and leave me alone. That is the struggle. It is the struggle to die to the false self. But this struggle is far, far beyond our own strength...Only in and through him can we survive the trails of our solitude...Only in the context of the great encounter with Jesus Christ himself can a real authentic struggle take place...We enter into solitude first of all to meet our Lord and to be with him and him alone...Only in the context of grace can we face our sin; only in the place of healing do we dare to show our wounds; only with a single-minded attention to Christ can we give up our clinging fears...As we come to realize that it is not we who live, but Christ who lives in us, that he is our true self, we can slowly let

our compulsions melt away and begin to experience the freedom of the children of God.
—Henri Nouwen (*The Way of the Heart* pg. 20-25)

We must create an intentional and either literal or figurative space of solitude to hear His still, small voice or great proclamation from heaven. These are pockets of time when we put off the false self, affirming what Christ demonstrated for us, to live out that God is the only source of our identity! To find freedom from the compulsions and temptations of our world to be relevant, spectacular, and powerful. We strive to be on Sabbath with the Lord in the quiet, free from the noise of distraction that seeks to invade our minds and our hearts and disrupts our peace.

When this doesn't happen, we get stuck in a cycle. The WHAT IF hamster wheel of life. Humans are, by nature, complex beings, and often get stuck and paralyzed, and we begin questioning ourselves because of these TWO words:

What IF!

We ask "what if" and question ourselves, our place, purpose, regrets, and wishes. They allow us to feel safe and protected. Initially, they provide a warm blanket that feels cozy. But staying safe in that comfort zone is precisely where the enemy wants us to stay. To stay safe, small, and limited, and believe that we control what's to come. Then we begin to justify, which puts us back in our comfort zone, creating a vicious cycle.

God didn't create you for that. We were all created to live life with peace and joy OVER fear!

"I leave the gift of peace with you—my peace. Not the kind of fragile peace given by the world, but my perfect peace. Don't yield to fear or be troubled in your hearts—instead, be courageous!" John 14:27 TPT

"I have told you this so that my joy may be in you and that your joy may be complete." John 15:11 NIV

We often feel that peace and abundant joy is slipping through our fingers. We have overwhelming rumblings during the "fullness of life" (a.k.a. busy, too much going on, chaos, rushing, commitments, to-do's, struggles). It's the fear and anxiety of what lurks outside the comfort zone. We struggle to tolerate the "rising" that comes with the unknown feeling outside that zone.

> "Thriving in God is only possible when we leap from comfort to discomfort!"
>
> *becky dozeman*

But we are invited to remember, it's outside this zone where God can use us most!

Outside of our comfort zone is where God meets us.

Remember the furnace of transformation that Nouwen shared with us? He meets us to burn away what isn't needed, to prune what doesn't serve, and promises that we are no longer the same.

Thriving in God is only possible when we leap from comfort to discomfort!

What did Jesus model?

Our Savior was the ultimate disruptor.

Christ was a rebel.

His presence shook up everything.

Jesus lived a life of stepping out into the unknown. HE was modeling, showing, and leading us to walk into the unknown rather than staying safe.

How many incredible ideas do you keep in a box or the corner of your heart?

How many lives remained unchanged because of just TWO words?

TWO simple words carry such power over us.

WHAT-IF…

Pause.

Reflect.

Deep breath.

I invite you to ask yourself:

- How often have I thought of these two words?
- How often have these two words kept me from trying, doing brave, and leaning in?
- How often have these words led me to believe that I can't do, shouldn't do, or that I am incapable of doing {fill in the blank}?

I have been held captive by these two words too. They have paralyzed me more than I want to admit. Our thoughts (for this example, the "what-if") create a belief, a narrative we listen to, formed by our experiences and stored memories.

Thoughts and subsequent beliefs created lead to an emotional rising (not just the feelings in our minds but the physiological experience of rapid heart rate, quickened breathing, warm face, headache, and belly flutters). Our body experiences the emotion first, then our minds, and we name that experience fear and anxiety.

Then the what-if is born!

We rehearse and play out why it won't work and we can't do it.

And then what do we do?

We do whatever it takes to make that all go away.

We halt.

We avoid.

We numb.

We distract.

We worry.

And then the world misses out on what God created you to do and be—your most genuine purpose in Him.

The idea stirring in you died because you had one thought: Oh, no… WHAT-IF?

It kept you from moving into what God had put on your heart.

My own WHAT-IF story started in the fall of 2020, as I cuddled up in my quiet time cozy spot with my favorite candle burning next to me. Those TWO words arose in my life like never before. My mind looped over them. The "what-if" reel played through my days and kept me awake at night. I had experienced the what-if multiple times before, but this was different. Life closed in around me, and I had to decide between giving up or leaning in. Those TWO words pulled and tugged on my weary soul.

I'd spent my entire career in the mental health world, most often in the role of therapist. It was an honor to hear stories and provide support. Unfortunately, the hard reality of others' stories became almost too much during the pandemic. As front-line mental health and helping professionals, it was common for us to begin feeling overwhelmed. It began to suffocate me. We weren't immune! I knew a change was necessary.

Like many of us at this time, all my mind could think was... WHAT-IF?

Only by God's grace, his consistent pursuit of my soul, and due to the patience that only He provides, I chose to lean in and battle with the "what-if." Honestly, I was afraid. Choosing brave, all the while still feeling the fear. I couldn't continue as I was. All that was left was to lean in, even though fear choked me.

What did I do? I did it scared, yet with God. I felt my fear and acted BRAVE, even though I didn't feel brave.

Even though the "what-if" questions bubbled up within me. I felt as though I was stumbling through a jungle blindfolded, trying to navigate a path to an unknown destination. I was distracted by the grip of perfectionistic tendencies. But I could no longer avoid the stirrings in my soul. There was a whispering in my mind that I needed to take my passion for helping others in a new direction. But I still needed to learn what that looked like, much less how to do it.

I got up early on the 1st Sunday in December 2020 for quiet time, a chance for Sabbath, to find solitude with the

Lord. I grabbed my devotional and realized that I had finished it previously that week and hadn't even noticed. So, I picked up the next one from my pile. Yes, I crave devotionals.

With the book in my lap, I prayed fervently, "Lord, I need you in this with me. I am thinking what-ifs and feeling all the fear… but you are so much bigger than that. I can't stay here, yet I am uncertain how to proceed. I know you tell us not to test you, so I am disobeying and asking for a sign. Please throw it in my face with complete clarity" (um, please know that God didn't have to answer me in my timing. He's in charge. We don't get to tell him what and when… honestly, I know He doesn't guarantee He'll appear in my human timeline.)

I ended my prayer and opened my new devotional, and it asked me to read Hebrews 11. It is the story of the faithful. It's the account of how God worked in the lives of our Old Testament friends.

> "Now faith is being sure of what we hope for and certain of what we do not see. This is what the ancients were commended for. By faith, we understand that the universe was formed at God's command, so what is seen is not made of what is visible." Hebrews 11: 1-2 NIV

God was clear. He took me on His lap, wrapped his arms around me, and whispered, "It's simple dear one-you, live this life by faith. I've got you." But I was still like, "Come on, Lord, this isn't the clarity I wanted. This isn't a clear-cut path. Where's the writing on the wall, the business plan, the assurance that it will all be okay?" "Dear one, you live this life by faith. You choose a free will path, but trust that I will guide your steps." I said yes amidst uncertainty, which required me to release control.

If you are like me and prefer certainty, then you get this. I love confidence, too. Please give me the ending, and I am all good. Accepting HIS invitation to trust was the best thing I could do, yet it is hard for us. I had the decision to make.

Either I choose to believe all of what God's love letter of the Bible declares, or I don't. It's all God-breathed and full of truth, or it isn't. Going through any experience in life alone isn't what God intends. We weren't created to do life solo. We were created to do life together and, even more importantly, to be together in the hard, the difficult, the unknown, and the seasons of uncertainty.

I knew I couldn't do it alone. What did I do? I leaned out on others for prayer support, practical support, business growth support, to have fun and distract me on non-workdays, and just the peace of knowing people were in my corner to help cheer me on and to problem-solve with me. Community and inviting others into our journeys, whether joyful or struggling, is always the best "yes." This will take authenticity and vulnerability, which might not always be comfortable, but practicing this skill will change how you live.

I engaged in what I NEEDED to find my way to living in my purpose and be valuable to my clients. First, I invested in ME because I know I can't serve my family or others if I am "empty." Then, I invested in pouring into MY BEST YESES! I increased my therapy sessions and hired a life and business coach. My nutrition, fitness, and other self-care practices became even more critical. They were now purpose-driven. I rested, napped, and chilled a LOT! I also told my people how I felt and what I needed because "clear is kind."

With nearly two decades of professional knowledge, training, and life experiences, my virtual coaching services for Christian women started to take form. After hosting virtual events, my coaching offerings evolved into a new and exciting design. Yes, as a new "entrepreneur," I had very few skills in running an actual business. The kind that requires you to do big girl things—create an LLC, find an accountant, open a business bank account, and more. God sent me the right people as I needed them, which provided a whole new vision. Although it was a significant life shift, I have found obeying God's calling easier.

My vision and mindset shifted from "Lord, what is my purpose? How can I serve others when I feel overwhelmed" to "Thank you, Lord, for my life experiences and challenges so that I can pursue what you have called me to do and live into my purpose." I felt all the feelings, but I chose, amidst fear, to lean in despite the "what-ifs." Then, I stayed in wonder with God! The awe of Him and the wonder of what we are creating together.

You won't believe it. This new adventure in my career has been amazing! Everything has been as good as I could have imagined for the past two-plus years. Everyone I have worked with was incredible. I figured out how to run a business overnight. There were no growing pains, and I have been on autopilot since then. I never struggle with the work-mom life rhythms, and it's been close to total and complete perfection.

Did you believe me? You know it wasn't. Stepping out in faith to become a business owner was so scary! I still, to this day, feel out of my league and barely know the difference between a W-2 and a W-9.

Instead of complete bliss, simplicity, and ease as described above, it was a TON OF WORK!

Not everyone supported me.

Not everyone interested in working with me chose to sign up.

Some people judged me.

Some people wanted me to fail.

Some of my staff and associates bailed mid-business creation.

Some of my closest friends shifted the way they felt about me.

One even called me a narcissist for being confident to do this.

My income was unstable, at best.

It was perfectly imperfect.

God did and is doing incredible things!

I have learned more about HIM, his WORD, myself, and what Christian women think, feel, need, do, and struggle with.

I have been blessed with the gift of creating a learning, growth, and expansion space.

By God's grace, I took the best of the private therapeutic process and married it to the proven benefits of a group experience. The group community is my favorite because when we have the chance to hear other women's stories, we are changed. When we experience, "Me too, I get that. I've felt that way,". When we hear stories of being brave, we are inspired.

What about you? What's your what-if?

What-if your what-if became... WHAT-IF NOT... or better yet...

I WONDER!

What if you do it scared, uncertain, and afraid?

You will change.

You will not remain the same.

You will change others' lives, too!

I wonder if your obedience will lead to God shining in the life of another!

Yet often, we question our choices.

What could we have done to avoid the doubting questions?

We question what's next.

There is so much growth and abundant learning in this season.

Find the gift in the hard.

How about a mindset shift too?

From "Why am I going through this?" TO "What is the learning? Show me the opportunity here, Lord!"

It will change everything. Shifting opposition to opportunity ignites hope in our minds. Our journey toward heaven rests in seeing our mental clutter differently. If you are doing it well (in alignment with God's will), you will and should hardly recognize yourself at various phases of your journey.

It's not about who you become in the end. It's about something other than the goals reached or unreached.

It's setting intentions daily and living out who you become on the way to the last chapter of your story. It's about "the learning" on the journey, not the destination. It's about who you become on the journey to where you are headed, ultimately our heavenly home. It's not about focusing on when, if, or how you get there because your path will most certainly shift. It's about who you become during your travels on that path that matters! Unfortunately, we get caught up in all the what-ifs of getting there or mastering that. While these can be beautiful pursuits, our focus is often on the ending when the space between today and heaven is the gift. It's the gift of your transformation on the path to where He's leading.

And at the end of the day, you chose to live out your brave… your life to-do list is much simpler.

The list is: to know him and to make him known.

And you know there are TWO ways this worry thing can go…

1) The fear/anxiety is a lie, and nothing terrible happened. Your worries didn't come true.

2) An issue arose, but it wasn't as bad as you thought, meaning you exaggerated it in your mind. You created an imaginary catastrophe. Also, you had the coping skills and resources to deal with it when it arose.

In a study called "Exposing Worry's Deceit" by Harvard University Research, participants recorded their worries online nightly for ten days. Then, they came back to track their reality across thirty days. What were the results?

- 91.4% of worries didn't come true.

- 8.6 % did and showed that when the problem did occur, it was manageable and not as bad as they had thought.[3]

The invitation is to reduce the chaos while we shift to soak up the truth. Rather than being stuck in the depths of mental clutter, we embrace the lessons God allows us to experience to live with mental, emotional, and spiritual clarity.

> "Do not conform to the pattern of this world but be transformed by the renewing of your mind. Then you can test and approve God's will—his good, pleasing, and perfect will." Romans 12:2 NIV

If you can shift the mental clutter, built from the foundation of lies and the "what-ifs," into grace-filled mental clarity, full of wonder and belief in the truth of who God says you are… then you are on the journey to abundance and thriving. God calls us to this as we journey to heaven.

You oversee your attention and awareness. You are still trying to figure out where to focus. God will reveal it to you… make intentional choices to focus on what matters most to God and your soul.

Abide in Him.

Dwell in His presence.

What awaits you on the other side is wisdom like no other. Rest assured, with God, you will find your "best yes." I wonder what that would be…

---

[3] LaFreniere LS, Newman MG. Exposing Worry's Deceit: Percentage of Untrue Worries in Generalized Anxiety Disorder Treatment. Behavioral Therapy. 2020 May, 51(3): 413-423.

What if you declared:

- I constantly move past "what if" fearing fear and into trusting God.
- I will bravely leave the "what ifs" behind me and invite in the transformational power of "I wonder"!

Be brave with yourself and complete these journal prompts:

- I fear…
- Because…
- When has fear and anxiety kept me from leaning into my brave…
- What's possible if I step toward my fears and anxiety to let God move in…
- -How would I feel if I lived more in the mindset of "I wonder" instead of "what-if"…

Prayer to God

Lord, I pray I no longer limit YOU! Either I believe you are who you say you are, trust that you are for me, and choose to develop a steadfast faith in YOU…or I don't.

Thank you for reminding me that perfection is reserved only for YOU. I am not included in the invitation to model perfection; your son Jesus has achieved that for me.

Any effort or focus I put forth "on being perfect" or "living captive in fear and anxiety" only widens the divide from YOU, my creator.

Help me break up with perfection, fear, and anxiety… as I aim to be more LIKE Christ.

Such abundant freedom is found when I release the drive to have it all figured out, shiny enough to let others see the authentic me.

Help me remember I am more beautiful to you in all my imperfections. Even though I stumble on the journey of faith, I choose to live in the "I wonder mindset" and abandon the fear-filled "what-if mindset." Therefore, the "what-ifs" no longer keep me in fear and uncertainty… YOU have overcome! When fear and anxiety are present, they are a catalyst to lean into YOUR word, will, and grace.

Amen!

Reflection

if they stumble
badly, they will
still survive, for the
Lord lifts them up
with his hands.

Psalm 37:23-26

I've got the joy!

Lori L. Dixon, Ed.S.

"Now may God, the fountain of hope, fill you to overflowing with uncontainable JOY and perfect peace as you trust him. And may the power of the Holy Spirit continually surround your life with his super-abundance until you radiate HOPE!" Romans 15:13, The Passion Translation

I've got the joy, joy, joy, joy down in my heart.
Where?
Down in my heart.
Where?
Down in my heart.
I've got the joy, joy, joy, joy down in my heart.
Down in my heart to stay.

And I'm so happy, so very happy.
I have the love of Jesus in my heart!
And I'm so happy, so very happy.
I have the love of Jesus in my heart!

Do you know this old song many of us sang as children in Sunday school and church?

I've been teaching it to my grandchildren, and it is so much fun!

I LOVE MUSIC!

> "God wants us to lift our voices into the heavens and bring the blessing of music AND joy onto the earth."
>
> *lori l. dixon*

I have a great friend whose daughter used to sing constantly from a young age. Driving her somewhere and sitting in the back seat, this little one would start singing songs. Some were her own that she had written or made up, and somewhere from school, church, or even the radio or music CDs. I loved hearing her sing, and now because of letting her express herself in such a profound way, she writes and performs her own music and is a performing arts academy. Best part? She loves GOD and is in a personal relationship with God!

God wants us to lift our voices into the heavens and bring the blessing of music AND joy onto the earth. So let's talk about JOY! As you read, you will see my chapter on "Balance and Bliss," where I believe you can find BLISS in everyday stuff. Bliss, for me, is the elevated level of JOY. So I dedicate this chapter to the profound joy I was around growing up to learn how to see, feel, and share it.

I have always felt the Holy Spirit in my praise and worship time. That intimate level of peace and calm, paired with exhilarating and lifting energy. Wow! That is BLISS! That is joy!

How did I learn such a relationship with joy and its understanding of how it was in my life? My mom! She was known for being filled with joy, and even though she sometimes struggled with her joy, she relied on her faith in God and Christ to fill her back up to overflowing enough for herself and enough to share with others. Whether it was friends, church, neighbors, or later, people who came to her work windows at Ivy's/Dillard's in Florida. They would all sit in that window where she managed the switchboard, announcements, and security, including the store manager. She was filled with love and joy for anyone who needed a quiet, listening ear or a joke of the day. Mom was even the implementer of morning trivia for all the employees working before the store opened. She was a guiding light for many through their challenges in life and love.

Mom "adopted" those that needed a mom, sister, or friend during her time on this earth, and her joy supported her in her struggles when she experienced the sudden loss of my dad.

I always saw the true character of my mom, especially as she grieved and learned to create a life without him since that wasn't their plan. My mom modeled for me and others how to read her bible, do her devotionals and absorb bible studies, and of course, church would keep her going and still sharing her JOY through her Lord.

After my dad had passed and my husband was working nights and weekends, it allowed time for Mom and me to take the periodic "getaway" girl trips. We loved traveling and driving to places we may have never been or simply wanted to enjoy firsthand. Many were beach trips because Mom and I adored the beach, and the peacefulness we felt there gave us much time to talk about memories and Dad. So, of course, that is why we all moved to Florida in 1981.

I have to share two major episodes of pure joy that I remember most with my mom. One trip was to our favorite hotel on St. Petersburg beach called The Tradewinds Hotel and Resort. The whole property was utterly amazing. It rested right on the beach with extended areas of its private beach to walk and collect shells. They had a small waterway for paddle boats and gondola rides. There were many outdoor areas for games, restaurants, gift shops, markets and delis, hammocks, and other serene seating for reading and the occasional nap space. There were two pools, jacuzzis, and water toys, attendants to help you with everything, including shaded chaise lounges, bungalows on the beach, and umbrellas. I remember every area of the resort and the shopping and restaurants within walking distance, too. My mom was a seasoned walker, and we would "walk and talk" for hours. I treasured those moments with her. Even to this day, they are ingrained within my brain.

Our hotel room was always extravagant with mini kitchens, great beds, and large bathrooms, and of course, our room always had a beach view with a balcony for sitting and eating as needed. We would bring food and stock our refrigerator with beverages, fun snacks, and lite bites to indulge in at sunset. Sometimes we would create a picnic or even buy a prepared one from the marketplace and then go down to the beach to walk and find a perfect spot for munching together and watching the sunsets. We would be up at sunrise walking the beach or playing around downstairs, go for a walk, and then find where we wanted to read, rest, and get sun for the day until lunch. What a perfect plan we would have for the long weekend! We were both readers and would share passages, laugh, chat about them, or even shed a tear when needed. A lot of healing would happen for both of us, for sure. We did devotions, bible reading, and prayer together daily. God was always part of our lives, no matter what had happened.

One particular long weekend, we had reservations at the Tradewinds. We couldn't wait! My husband (the first one) was working all weekend on inventory. He was a general manager for a major restaurant chain, and I knew what that would be like for him. I wanted to be away. He and I had a strange relationship, and he wasn't involved much from the beginning. But that's a story for another time. Going away with Mom was a much-needed experience. Her joy everywhere we went was contagious. I loved that about her.

We packed and met at my house, closer to our drive to St. Pete Beach. Mom looked at the newspaper and said, "The weather report for the weekend isn't expected to be favorable for a beach weekend." I asked her, "What does that mean? I don't believe it anyway. They are always wrong." Her face scrunched up, and her fingers moved like that of rain and wind. I shook my head no. We both prayed all the way to the beach for GREAT sun and calm weather. The first night was perfect. The day was filled with cool breezes, a steel drum band on the beach, and a breathtaking sunset, and we were filled with sensory moments that led to a great night's sleep. We even opened the sliding door to hear the waves crashing and the seagulls singing.

The following day we got up at sunrise like usual, and while there was a bit of cloudiness, we would not let it stop our walk on the beach or our lounging with great books for the day. We got dressed and packed up. As we walked through the resort, we heard everyone talking about the heavy rain expected with harsh winds coming in. We let them all know that these storms often pass right over us, being right on the beach the way we were. Some locals agreed, and the staff also verified our thoughts. We continued our routine, picked up some breakfast and coffee, and headed to find our beach chairs in our familiar spot. It was so safe then that you could leave your bags on your chairs, and the attendants would watch them for you. Leaving our beach bags and cooler, we grabbed our small wallets and walked down the beach. Mom and I would walk a little and then stop for a bit. In one of our "sit down" moments, we both said, "Those clouds are not moving away, and it is getting a little darker." Yes, the acknowledgment was vital at this moment. We decided to turn around and walk back on the long walk to the resort and where our beach chairs were. At least, as a preventative measure, we put the umbrella covers over our two chairs for safety.

With each step closer to our destination, we would remark about the people moving off the beach and the huts closing, too. Hum? Maybe they knew something we didn't know. We walked at a little faster pace as we were about half a mile away. At least we could see the hotel and knew where we were going. Hotel by hotel we passed, they were closing up their outdoor items and retreating inside. Mom and I looked at each other and sped up a little more. Then, it started. Confirmation that it would rain was now a reality, and the sprinkles were okay until the breeze turned into more of a wind. The wind got even stronger, cooler temperatures, and the rain was now falling hard. It was raining, and Mom and I could only move quicker with the gusts of the wind and laugh. As we approached our resort, people were on their balconies cheering us on, the only people on the beach. It was pouring down rain, and Mom and I looked like drowned and cold rats, and we knew it. We waved and thanked our cheerleaders and laughed hysterically as we picked up our dry and safe beach bags to run for cover in the resort. The staff was laughing, too, knowing we disagreed with their weather predictions, but they giggled as they helped us inside to safety. Mom and I laughed the entire walk to our room to take much-needed hot showers. We talked with our cheerleader onlookers the whole time we were there, and everyone enjoyed what happened—a memory in the making for everyone.

We agreed God is good in anything! Rain or shine, his joy, and blessings continue to be abundant, even in the abundance of RAIN and WIND. We knew God could have stopped the rain for us, and we knew he could have created another perfect beach day for all of us. But because of this occurrence and our reaction to it, JOY was the outcome, and people were affected by our walk. When others asked us why we didn't come in sooner, we told them God had us covered, and he is always good. Many would nod, and some would agree out loud. God was glorified, even in Mom's, and my grief of losing Dad and JOY abounded.

Are you beginning to see the need for JOY in your life? Do you feel that JOY is possible even during hardship, grief, obstacles, and just life occurrences? God is there!

Now, for the second story. I shared that my mom and I enjoyed these long weekends and sometimes longer getaways. Living in Florida allowed us to travel to many fun and "flavorful" locations. My mom loved fruits and vegetables! She grew up on a farm, and when we lived in Illinois, a garden was always a big part of our big yard, along with many flower beds and bushes or fragrant aromas. Part of my responsibilities growing up was to help her work in the garden from seed to harvest, so I knew the span of our labor well. Mom and Dad always loved peppers, onions, cucumbers, tomatoes, carrots, celery, radishes, and green beans. Imagine what great salads and dishes could be made from these fresh vegetables for our family. Did I say mom and dad loved onions? Well, they did, so much so that mom would bite into a freshly picked purple onion and eat it from the garden. Of course, you can imagine my reaction! Yuck! And I would run away from her so I didn't have to smell that smell. It is probably why I am a vegetarian/primarily vegan now. I loved our garden.

When we all moved to Florida, Mom, and Dad didn't plan a garden anymore. They did have the most beautiful flowers and yard, though. Mom always picked fresh flowers for the house, and the fragrance of gardenia and jasmine to this day are my favorites. After Dad passed, Mom and I continued taking our getaways together, and fruit and vegetables were always part of our agenda. We'd often go to the strawberry fields and festivals in Plant City, where most of the strawberries in our area come from, or the orange groves around us to pick fresh juices. Mom always wanted to support the small and local growers, and my husband and I still do this now.

One such trip every year was to Georgia, Valdosta, to be exact. Do you know what comes from that area? Vidalia ONIONS, of course, PEACHES, and PECANS, yes! Plus, even more, amazing produce we only sometimes had in Florida. I loved their cantaloupe and watermelon, too. By the way, my first garden at four years old was a watermelon and pumpkin. Back to the story… we had to go to Georgia every year at just the right harvest time for these precious items in our family. This particular year was no different in our search for the perfect produce stand or farm store. We would drive up the highway and begin sampling. Each highway exit had a hand-drawn sign for whatever they were selling. Mom knew, I think by instinct and, yes, smell, where we needed to stop. She would say, "Don't bother stopping." others would say, "Pull over now!" I would likely oblige. What a trip we were making, winding around the twists, turns, and exits of the highway before us up through Georgia. Each night we stayed at a fun and nice hotel, it was really to sample the "goods" in our room and plan the next day of shopping. Mom knew how many of each coveted fruit or veggie she wanted to have as we wound our way back to Florida. We would rate each item and then list the exit and when we needed to pull off to purchase our amount to fill our trunk with freshness.

One particular evening after a long day of driving, eating, stopping, and driving some more, Mom and I decided to treat ourselves to a nice dinner and hotel. Little did I know that after the exhaustion of shopping for produce, I would be awakened in the middle of the night. Right before bed, we decided to share a luscious peach. When you cut it, this was the kind that squirts its flavorful juice onto the plate. Then, when you bite into it, the juiciness runs down your chin to be caught by a hopefully available napkin. If the peaches we purchased each day didn't have the juiciness factor paired with the unbelievable sweetness to match, we didn't go back for more.

After eating and truly enjoying one of the best peaches we had found, we agreed to go to bed and return to that stand the next day. We fell deeply asleep after the long day and sweet dessert. Well, at least I thought WE were both sleeping.

Around midnight, I heard my mom say, "Lori, what was that?" in a somewhat scared voice.

It woke me from a wonderful dream, and I said, "Mom, I don't know. I don't hear anything."

She proceeded to say, "Don't you hear it? There are voices!"

Now, I am beginning to wonder about my mom's sanity in the middle of the night. Maybe the sugar had affected her badly in some way. I was fully awake to make sure she was okay. "Mom, I don't hear anything. Are you okay?"

She quickly responded, "Lori, there it is again! Those peaches are calling me... don't you hear them..."

Oh, my gosh! Was she serious? Now, when she repeated it, I said, "Mom, are you hearing the peaches?"

She jumped out of bed and said, "Yes! They are calling me to eat them!" We both jumped up and started laughing so loudly together and talking about how I thought she was serious. That made us laugh even more!

The next day, I told her we had to listen to the peaches before we bought them just to make sure they were the talking kind. We both couldn't help but laugh and did so all the way home. Did we find more talking peaches? I don't know, but they were almost all eaten on the drive back, so they must have been the right ones.

We walked into the house with our arms filled with Vidalia sweet onions, pecans, cantaloupe, and of course, peaches. It was a GOOD trip! Mom shared some with me, and I drove home knowing I would treasure this crazy, silly trip forever... and I have!

> "I am a true sprouting vine, and my Father is the farmer who tends the vine. He cares for the branches connected to me by lifting and propping up the fruitless branches and pruning every fruitful branch to yield a great harvest. The words I have spoken over you have already cleansed you. So you must remain in life-union with me, for I remain in life union with you. But if you live in union with me and if my l words live powerfully within you—then you can ask whatever you desire and it will be done. "When your lives bear abundant fruit, you demonstrate that you are my mature disciples who glorify my Father. ... My purpose for telling you this is so that the JOY that I experience will fill your hearts to overflowing gladness!" John 15:1-4, 7-8; The Passion Translation

Joy can be in silly stories you share and in the moments you treasure for God's glory. My memories of my family are surrounded not only by the love I have for them but the faith we share, the prayers we say to honor our relationship with God, the hysterical moments with our grandchildren, and the JOY God has bestowed on us to assist in the difficult times of life.

God loves us...not just in our stoic and serious times, but also in our joyful and worship-filled breaths taken while praising Him. Making God the center of your life is vital to unlocking how you see everything in its newness and completeness of his actions and grace for us. We are His children! He laughs with us and weeps with us, too. We are HIS!

Prayer to God

Thank you for the memories of pure joy and laughter even in life's difficulties, Lord. We know you are always there for us and with us! Thank you for the friends and family to spend special times with in our lives. Thank you for the bountiful harvest of the fruits and vegetables in our life, especially peaches. May we walk in the seasons we face, Lord, hand in hand with you, sitting down when needed and running at other times. May we realize the fruits of the Spirit we are to embrace in our life of goodness, faithfulness, compassion, …

May the JOY we feel in the Lord be realized by those around us to glorify His name and bring purpose and passion to the lives of those who feel and hear. May we be the instruments for God's Kingdom daily in our weaknesses and strengths. Amen.

Reflection

May God, the fountain of hope, fill you to overflowing with uncontainable joy

Romans 15:13

is this my life?

Molly Brown

"And let us not be weary in well-doing: *for in due season we shall reap, if we faint not.*" Galatians 6:9 ASV

I am a follower of Christ. I was saved a long time ago. I have been a leader at church, hosted bible studies, served in several areas, and prayed on behalf of others. I am normal! I have a social life and probably too many hobbies. I am successful! I am a counselor with a master's degree. I am loved! I have a wonderful family and so many dear friends. But I sat up all night on the tenth floor of the county hospital, an infamous locked-down psychiatry unit, continuously asking myself, "How is this my life?"

That night, I was handcuffed and taken in the back of the SUV downtown like a criminal. I was not coping well, but I was not suicidal that night. I was triggered and reached out to friends who assured me I could call and ask for help anytime. I just wanted someone to be there, and to sit with me for a while before I went to sleep next to my companion, my English bulldog Raji. The hospital experience added another layer of trauma to the tangled web of terror I had been fighting for almost a year. As the hours passed and I could not hold it any longer, I got up to go to the shared restroom, only to find semen all over the toilet seat. A woman walked around the room, tapping people throughout the night while she muttered to herself. A man walked in circles in front of me, glancing at me regularly. I could feel demonic spirits and see them in his eyes. I prayed and sang worship songs to myself to fight the battle clearly orchestrated by Satan.

When I asked to be seated away from the crowd, my option was the tiny "women-only" room. There, I covered my ears from the violent screaming and cursing of a woman who had lost touch with reality before she tried to escape the unit. It was heartbreaking and downright terrifying. In the early hours of the morning, the staff brought out breakfast. Eggs. Recalling the painful experience of being hospitalized for and surviving two blood clots in my lung following six months of cancer treatment to rid my body of stage four Lymphoma a few years before, I began gagging from the familiar smell and clear traumatic memories. I dry-heaved until breakfast was over, and the trays had been cleared from the room.

I had been up all night and had not seen a doctor to explain my situation. I was ignored by a nurse in the morning when I tried to seek more information about the nightlong wait and anticipated time to be seen. When I was able to ask her again when I could be seen, she rolled her eyes and told me I could take something to "remain calm." It took an entire night awake before someone would listen to my story and allow me to go home.

By the time I was released from the hospital into freedom and fresh air, I had sat awake for what seemed like forever, been forced to take my clothes off and change in front of male medical personnel, and seen nurses and a doctor. Yet, my stomach and legs were still sticky with dried blood from cutting myself the night before, and I was heading home with new trauma.

In the summer of 2018, I had been happily married for six years, was a proud and thankful cancer survivor, a follower of Jesus and active in church, successful in my career, with wonderful family and friends, and I was seemingly quite content in life. The flashbacks started in the middle of the night throughout the summer and into the fall. As I pieced together the memories of a sexual assault years before that my brain had blacked out for so long, I began to change. Anxiety crept its way inside, I suppressed intense feelings of shame and depression, I began to withdraw from friends and family, I replaced nightly reading and tea time with boxed wine and mindless television shows to cope, and I began to act completely unlike myself. The thoughts and behaviors finally brought me to a breaking point, and following a yoga class one Wednesday evening, I came home and told my husband I wanted to die.

He sought the help of some of our godly friends, and my mom flew down from Wisconsin. The next few days were a blur, and I fell asleep crying aloud about wanting to die. I knew why I felt that way, I had a plan and means to end my life, and I felt utterly broken and hopeless. I started seeing a therapist in the days that followed who helped me begin to process what happened, my behavior, and my intrusive thoughts, but my marriage was deeply suffering. It was up and down for the next few months, as was my mental health. My husband decided to move ahead with a divorce in April. I kept thinking, "Is this really my life?" It took months for the shock to subside. I have always moved through difficult seasons by "pulling up my bootstraps" and deflecting any true feelings of pain. I thought I was ok; I had a strong support system through my family, friends, and my therapist, but time proved I was far from any version of ok.

I continued to spiral and act uncharacteristically out of control. I was simply trying to survive. I self-harmed more and more and considered ending my life on several occasions. I could not possibly imagine a resolution to walking through traumatic memories, poor decisions, a divorce, strained or ruined relationships, debt, rejection, shame, embarrassment, regret, and extremely intense and incredible self-hatred. The events that unfolded following the night in the hospital compounded the weight I was carrying, and it nearly crushed me. I fantasized about ending my life anytime I was triggered, which was often. Could I successfully hang myself from my ceiling fan, balcony, or showerhead? How long would my dog be waiting at my side until someone found me? He would be sad, of course, but no one else would care. After putting a rope around my neck and pulling tight to test my plan, I decided that pain was not how I wanted to end my life, so I decided when it was time, I would go back to my original plan of pills so I could feel nothing. My dog, Raji, had always been by my side, so at one point, I bargained with myself that I would try to wait until he passed on to kill myself.

Time went on, COVID-19 entered the world, and I spent several months in Wisconsin with my parents, the most loving and supportive people I have ever known. They have seen me at my lowest and loved me unconditionally and nonjudgmentally. Without their selfless care for me, I would not still be alive. I diligently continued therapy once a week, sometimes twice, when I knew I was really struggling. I progressed at times and was setback many others, and through it, I continued to wonder, "Is this seriously my life?"

One of the most challenging things in walking through this journey is feeling like I must hide it, along with the shame, embarrassment, and fear that travels with such a "secret." In moments of suicidal ideation and the processing afterward, my heart would ache because I felt like a fake. I may be the last person one would ever expect to be suicidal. No one would suspect I could be so regularly in such a dark place. Yet, I am so cheery, silly, positive, compassionate, encouraging, outgoing, and vibrant. While those aspects of my personality are completely honest, authentic, and apparent, I also struggle with major depression, anxiety, self-harm, and suicidal ideation. I was and still am so grateful for the outpouring of love and support as I was battling stage four cancer several years ago. Still, some moments during my ongoing mental health journey have made it feel almost impossible to share this experience with anyone outside my immediate circle for support. Though mental health awareness has gained some attention and respect, the world has a long way to go with understanding and nonjudgmentally supporting those who have or are struggling with mental health concerns.

"I am the chosen daughter of the most high King."

molly brown

I had processed how difficult it was to fight for my life while going through cancer treatment and chemotherapy and how inexplicably more challenging and exhausting it had been to fight for my life throughout the past few years when I was otherwise so seemingly physically healthy. I have even wished at times that I had died from cancer. *It is one thing to fight for your life when you want to live, and it is another entirely different war to fight for your life when everything in you screams that you want to die.*

May 12, 2021—I decided the next day, my birthday, would be the perfect day to leave the earth. I thought, "How is this the end of my life?" But God had other plans. While my walk has parts of intense heartache and raw struggle, God's presence can be seen in every step. He is where hope and healing are found. That night, my neighbor stopped by with some of my favorite foods to wish me a happy birthday after a business dinner. Afterward, I had an emergency evening appointment with my therapist, who I genuinely believe is an angel from the Lord living on earth. I went to bed that night, feeling a glimmer of hope. The next day, I was showered with love from family and friends, and it was one of the best birthdays I can remember.

My journey has been, and continues to be, incredibly difficult, yet I continue to walk forward, even if it is a half-step at times. I am healing but imperfect, and I may wrestle with depression and anxiety at times for the remainder of my life on this side of Heaven. But as Lamentations 3:22-23 says, "The faithful love of the Lord never ends. His mercies never cease. Great is his faithfulness; his mercies begin afresh each morning." For every traumatic moment, every painful circumstance, every poor choice and struggle with sin, every heartache, every instance of self-harm, and every thought of suicide, I can testify with joy, confidence, faith, and hope how God forgives, doubly blesses and prevails each day. He has placed community in my life to love unconditionally, encourage, support, and patiently continue to care for me even when I have had no energy or ability to care for myself or reciprocate their time, compassion, and care. I am alive because my community has loved me how God has led them.

A friend even coined herself my "Guardian Gifter." For months, she would anonymously send encouraging and godly gifts that seemed to come during especially difficult moments or days when I needed love and hope the most. Not everyone with whom God has blessed me is human. My bulldog Raji knew it all. He saw it all. He was my companion through it all. Our bond is like no other, and I wholeheartedly believe he saved my life on several occasions and stayed here on earth until he knew I would be ok. When he passed not long after suddenly becoming ill, I was heartbroken. Satan reminded me of the plan to live only as long as Raji lived, but God prevailed again. He walked me through the heartache, later introduced me to, and blessed me with another spunky four-legged girl from a puppy mill who just wants a loving life. I named her Maggie after my favorite tree, the magnolia.

God has also blessed me with opportunities and experiences. Yoga has been a truly healing practice for my mind, emotions, and body. As I practiced more, I pondered the idea of sharing the healing practice with others. In June of 2021, I earned a yoga teaching certification. Throughout my yoga instructor training, I discovered more self-discipline, determination, and strength. Teaching yoga has been one of the most rewarding opportunities and has brought the sweetest community. I also closed one chapter in my career and opened another by pursuing a new professional position. I feared the change, the unknown, and the entailed insecurity. Still, God taught me humility and helped me develop confidence, assertiveness, and many more invaluable new skills through that step in faith. God has timely blessed me with freedom and space to travel and explore, too, taking a break from everyday life with family and friends to help me reset and feel refreshed.

My neighbor, who delivered some of my favorite foods on my birthday, became my best friend and partner. He helped me discover happiness and hope for the future when I did not know if it was possible again, and I am grateful for our story. I have experienced healing from an ongoing trusting and compassionate client-therapist relationship. I have seen God move through my therapist to patiently help me open the doors to and walk through past trauma, heartache, anger, shame, self-hatred, and every other feeling, emotion, and experience toward a direction of healing and wholeness. She has created a space where I can finally feel safe in the depths of my chaos.

This is my life. This is *a season of* my life. I have walked through it with God by my side every step of the way, even when I did not always feel it and even when fighting him in it. It has not been a quick or easy season, but the community, blessings, and opportunities revealed on the walk have developed wisdom within worth every moment. Wisdom to choose life. Wisdom to know God's mercy, goodness, and faithfulness. Wisdom to reject the lies of the enemy. Wisdom to surrender sin and what I cannot change. Wisdom to forgive myself and others. Wisdom to exceedingly practice gratitude. Wisdom to love extravagantly. Wisdom to boldly and humbly own my story. Wisdom to trust God in all things. And finally, wisdom to walk joyfully toward a new season in healing and wholeness as a chosen daughter of the most high King.

"I remain confident of this: I will see the goodness of the LORD in the land of the living." Psalm 27:13 NIV

To the reader, if you are processing trauma, have thoughts of hopelessness, experienced self-harm and/or suicidal ideation, and struggle with self-hatred, shame, loneliness, or rejection, the following prayer is especially for you to pray aloud as often as you need. Continue to seek the comfort of God, and connect with community because you, my friend, are not alone.

Prayer to God

Lord, thank you for your faithfulness. Thank you for your new mercies each and every morning. You know I am imperfect, yet you have covered my sin on the cross, and I am perfect to you. I repent of and release my imperfections to you, and I ask you to heal the areas of pain in my life, Lord. (Call out every area of pain in which you need healing.) I surrender, and I choose healing by the power of the Holy Spirit that raised Christ from the dead. I choose life. I choose peace. I choose mercy. I choose grace. I choose forgiveness for others and myself. I choose the wisdom and revelation from a relationship and the walk with you. I am safe now. I am your daughter, and I am your favorite. I trust the areas of pain in my life will be replaced with double the blessing because you are good. You are faithful. Your mercies never cease. Praise Jesus! Amen.

Reflection

I will see the goodness of the Lord in the land of the living.

Psalm 27:13

what's in your cup?

Lori L. Dixon, Ed.S.

This morning, I looked down tiredly into my cup. It was warm to my touch, and the beverage inside was luscious and yet bold at the same time. The flavor was that of light cherries, coconut, and COFFEE. It has that distinct smell, even when you don't drink it yourself. Today it was a blend of chocolate brownie and cherry cordial. Oh yes! It was like a dessert in a cup.

Coffee soothes me in the morning and reminds me of years gone by, sitting at the kitchen table with my mom and dad, who loved their coffee every day. Mom had the old percolator-type coffee pot when I was growing up until she moved to the drip kind many years later. Recently, when I became tired of the new machines with the excessive little cups, some of which you can recycle and some you cannot, I bought a percolator. When I opened the box, I couldn't believe it! It was like a flash from the past of the silver metal body, the black lacquer handle and bottom, and the little silver lid with the glass "see-through" top like a dome. That dome is where the coffee got pushed up and through to create the coffee pressure necessary for a robust flavor. It was a whole sensory experience that I now look forward to every morning.

I started loving coffee as a young child, yes… really! My mom's father was Danish and even taught me Danish Dansk words as I was growing up. Grandpa loved coffee and drank it all day. He said it reminded him of his family, coming over on a ship as a teenager and seeing others drink coffee, too. Grandpa wanted me to learn to like a beverage from his heritage, so every time we visited, I was given my own little cup of steamed milk, a little sugar, and the hot, black stuff until it reached the top. I couldn't wait to sit at the table and have coffee with all the adults. What a rite of passage that was for a young child.

Today, I look down at the cup, and I see the creamy caramel look on it. I breathe it in slowly, and I take a sip. What I didn't share with you was the cup. Not any cup, as some may think or choose. I was raised with a mom who collected mugs. They hung in her kitchen in every house we lived on the wall suspended on wooden hooks of a latticework structure. Mugs from places we had traveled, ones with scriptures, some with sayings like "One beautiful person and one old grump live here." That one was a joke between mom and dad that hung on the wall long after he was gone. Whenever I went anywhere, I bought mom a mug to remember my travels and let her know she was with me. When morning came, she chose a mug. Then her half-and-half was taken out of the refrigerator and added with one sweetener since now she had diabetes.

Mom would pour her cream in, add the coffee to just the desired color, and add only a ½ packet of the sweet substance. Then, she would sit down and do her devotional every morning.

Not only was I trained in how coffee should be drunk, the choice of a cup it would be placed in, and how you shared that savory experience with God. This ritual was the same until my mom could not come down the stairs in our home for her coffee time with me. The order in which we place things in life is how we "honor" them. So mom honored coffee…and she honored and glorified God, putting him in the right place and at the right time of her day… every day.

Today, I chose a mug with the ocean on it. We purchased it in Hawaii, which I love because of the memories it holds for me. I made coffee, added unsweetened coconut milk (my choice these days), and added no sweetness to my cup. Then, I walk to the table to read the next verses in the Bible and the chapter I am reading. I linger to breathe in the smoothness of the flavors, thank God for these moments each morning, and share my intentions for the day ahead as I dedicate them to His service. "May I be a support to others? May they know my heart and spirit are aligned with you."

God has me look at my cup today for some reason. He tells me that every action we do is an honor and moment with and for Him. He continues to provide the context of how the cup or mug matters and what we put inside it daily. Are we filled with exhaustion, haughtiness, ego-centric thoughts and actions, and self-fulfillment, or are we filled with compassion, love, gentleness, patience, and joy for others? I sit back and contemplate what God is saying today. I journal my thoughts and ideas for myself and my clients today. God is preparing me to walk in his wisdom forward today. Once my cup is finished, what will my thoughts be?

> "How can I grow my gifts even further for him so that my cup flows over in abundance every day?"
>
> *lori l. dixon*

Will what God has instilled in me be used for good in this world? How can I grow my gifts even further for him so that my cup flows over in abundance every day?

The cup...my cup overflowing...

In Psalm 23, David uses this expression to help us understand the abounding and overflowing nature of God's presence, provision, protection, and power. The blessing placed upon David wasn't just for his life, but it was designed to spill over so it could bless others. Isn't it the same for us?

The Cup... I share with you...

Jesus passed the cup of common drink to his closest followers and brothers. The cup was the symbolic chalice of a ritual of their faith filled with a beverage that may have been usual, yet its meaning would be felt for thousands of years and still true today. Take the cup, drink, and remember.

Jesus asked God, "... let this cup pass from me... is there any other way that we can accomplish what you want from me at this time..." He didn't wrestle with God; he fulfilled a prophecy set from past years. The "cup" was the cross. It is like me remembering my grandfather's words and teachings. Christ was fulfilling God's and the prophets before him as they shared words of his coming. It may be a simplistic way to consider the cup, yet isn't it sometimes the fundamental way we can understand things even better?

The cup… the drink… the ritual of our lives…

So, I ask you, does it matter? Does it matter what is in the cup you drink every day, the cup you choose, the pattern of ritual you may do to honor your Heavenly Father? God fills every cup "in him" to overflowing. Thou shall not thirst but have abundance in Him. Valuing what is IN the cup and not worrying or doubting whether it is half full or half empty, too. It is always filled, and the value of the beverage cannot be seen as lacking in quality or quantity.

> "Endless love beyond measurement that transcends our understanding—this extravagant love pours into you until you are filled to overflowing with the fullness of God." Ephesians 3:20 The Passion Translation

Prayer to God

God, remind us to honor the cup, the container we hold important things we treasure daily. May we honor you in each cup through each beverage we choose to enjoy. Let us remember to have precious time with you in a meaningful way, with that we hold most dear. Let us honor the memories of times and people that have since passed or moved on. Let their impact on us be great, only if it glorifies the life we lead for you to establish the Kingdom on earth for all that serve you. Thank you for each cup and each drink you provide for us in life.

Amen.

PS… I love tea, too, but that's a whole other conversation.

Reflection

this extravagant love pours into you until you are filled to overflowing with the fullness of God

Ephesians 3:20

shine, don't shrink

Irum Rashid-Jones

"And through his creative expression, this Living Expression made all things, for nothing has existence apart from Him! A fountain of life was in him, for his life is a light for all humanity. And this light never fails to shine through the darkness. A light that darkness could not overcome!" John 1:3-5 TPT

I have always wanted to shrink for as long as I can remember, even as a young child. I grew up in an environment where being unseen, unheard, and less of a burden was a form of obedience. See, I never had a chance to experience childhood. When I was four years old, I remember little Irum following someone down a dark hallway of an orphanage in the Middle East, and I couldn't help but feel a sense of confusion and betrayal—How did I end up here, in a place for abandoned children, when I know my parents are still alive? Did they forget about me? Was I such a naughty daughter that they gave me up because I didn't listen? These thoughts flooded my mind as I somehow decided that from this moment forward, I would never be able to play with my dolls again.

The feeling of abandonment was a badge I didn't want to wear, but I didn't have a choice. I remember telling myself every night, "Irum, one day you'll become an adult, and this deep sadness will just be a thing of the past...." I was only four years old at the time.

Eventually, I reunited with my family, but I was so wounded by being abandoned so early that I was too scared to embrace the childhood before me. I was never the same again. Instead of playing like most children, I washed pots in the kitchen and gave away my toys and treats, trying to earn my keep so that I wasn't thrown away again. I was so scared of being thrown away. I feared the dark because I remembered being taken away at night. I was too afraid to sleep because I thought if I did, then I would wake up again in a place where no one wanted me. I was only five years old. Being abandoned again was my greatest fear, and the characteristic of "earning my keep" followed me throughout my entire life, even leading into my teens.

Then as a teenager, I was abandoned again. This time I felt like I was tossed out, like a piece of garbage. Just like that, I became a nameless person that no one seemed to want. People mispronounced my name, called me by a different name, or said no name as if I wasn't there. I was no longer Irum, meaning in Arabic, "the person that lives in paradise and shines a brilliant bright light." Instead, I was whisked into one of the world's most brutal, darkest foster care systems, where only 2% of girls are lucky enough to survive. I didn't realize then that I would spend the next four years of high school bouncing back and forth between forty different foster homes.... I was now officially a "ward of the state" or what most people would refer to as a "foster child," a "problem child," or a "burden of society," someone "lost, unseen, or unworthy." Did I even matter?

The tiny voice inside my head reinforced and reminded me daily that to survive, I had to embrace the most arduous road ahead and that I would have to face it alone. I felt even more abandoned with each new home when my foster parents traded me for a younger child. Unfortunately, that's all I knew for the first 18 years. Each time the wound would get bigger, deeper, and more painful. Eventually, I started covering my wounds and pretending they weren't there. As women, we've become comfortable with having wounds and hiding them. Little did I know I would need to show them later in life to allow them to heal.

I thought, "Girl, if you focus all your energy on becoming a perfectionist, perfection will become your superpower. Work hard behind the scenes! Use it in your career, skills, projects, and every aspect of your life and relationships! Work quietly, play it safe, don't ruffle feathers, don't shine too much, don't make too much noise, and be as accommodating as possible." But, underneath it, all was perfectionism, coupled with a double dose of abandonment, unhealed wounds, and people-pleasing. It was a pathway to instability and addiction that would only allow me to shrink even further.

I spent years playing it safe, shrinking even more instead of shining, but that was all about to change when I decided to venture into entrepreneurship. Not only did I choose to enter a male-dominated industry like Construction, but there needed to be a community of women or a sisterhood of women entrepreneurs that I could lean on. It seemed like the road ahead would be lonely again - but this time, it was a road I chose.

Life as an entrepreneur isn't for the weak, but it's also one of the loneliest journeys I've traveled. Only a few people walk it. Let's get real—only a few *women* walk it. Many people quit the journey before it even gets started. So, what stopped me from quitting? Why did I decide to continue walking the path? Why did God put such a passion in my heart to continue the walk?

My roots and past? I remember the days I just wanted to quit. During those moments of doubt, I would recall my last journey, always beginning in a place of darkness. Yet, with time and perseverance, I hoped to find tiny sparks of light to guide me through this new part of the journey. Determined to find a spark or a shiny rock on the path, I developed a supernatural talent for perseverance that allowed me to continue, and I outpace my goals.

One year, my company received an award in a category that required an interview and a big celebration. For months,

I debated conducting the interview. I felt so out of place. I didn't want to be in the spotlight…

I didn't want to shine…

I didn't think I was worthy of shining…

Even though collectively, the company and every single person worked so hard, I knew I didn't have the strength for the awards ceremony. Why? Although on the outside, my confidence in my work, my skills, and my abilities was at a mastery level, the wounds from my past that I was covering up didn't heal. So I felt unworthy of healing and focusing my attention on shining.

Sometimes we shrink because we tell ourselves, "I don't want to be hurt anymore," or sometimes, we shrink. After all, it's safer or easier to shrink than to shine.

> "We are reborn into a perfect inheritance that can never perish, never be defiled, and never diminish. It is promised and preserved forever in the heavenly realm for you!" 1 Peter 1:4 TPT

It was as if my wounds were re-infected, and I wouldn't allow myself to shine. I wasn't taking care of my injuries. I was ignoring them. Why wouldn't my wounds heal on their own?

Do you feel like this?

Unworthy of shining?

Have you ever ignored your wounds?

Mine held me back, and I was too scared to allow them to heal. Finally, I didn't want to be hurt anymore and felt it would be better to leave them alone.

Have you ever felt that way?

Have you ever said to yourself, "God, can I just do it my way? If I ignore the pain, it will go away."

Your wounds won't heal independently because something deeper requires our attention. With God's promise and power, you'll heal faster. He will heal with wholeness. Please don't make the mistake that I made of leaving the wounds alone by covering them up.

Can I let you in on a secret? Did you know as Christians, we are called to shine bright and be a light to the world, reflecting the love and truth of God to those around us?

Then, why was I going through life shrinking on purpose instead of shining?

Why are YOU going through life shrinking on purpose instead of shining?

God has given us a promise.

> "Arise, shine, for your light has come, and the glory of the Lord rises upon you." Isaiah 60:1

I remember reading this scripture and thinking, "Irum, God has commanded every person to SHINE, yet YOU still refuse to embrace the light within you! So God is telling you at this very moment, by encouraging YOU to rise and shine YOUR light for the glory of God is upon every single one of us!" As I meditated on his word, I was so moved and motivated to shine as God has commanded us to shine and help others shine in their journeys.

Daily I meditated on shining more instead of shrinking and rolling up my sleeves to show my wounds, embracing my scars, and preparing for a journey ahead. A different journey this time that didn't allow me to shrink. A journey that was going to be filled with light and preparation that there were no guarantees—I might get hurt again. I might have new wounds to heal… but I was going to do something different for the first time in my life… I was going to shine…

How many times has your journey started in a dark place?

It's supposed to be dark when you start. That's why we feel every bump in the road: we're all walking in the dark, tripping over one another and stumbling over every stone. But maybe God needs just one of us on the path brave enough to shine so others on the same course can see us shine too.

Maybe God needs us to continue shining to motivate others along their path because let's face it—it's so easy to quit! Maybe God is telling you right now that you need to quit "quitting" on yourself, and instead of shrinking—SHINE! This dark road ahead may become a beautifully lighted path that isn't lonely anymore because we have all found one another and are shining for each other.

Is that what God needed me to do? "God, is that what you need me to do?" YES!

Is that what God is telling you to do right now? YES!

SHINE, don't shrink!

Remember, as we walk and grow in our faith, our light will shine brighter and brighter, illuminating the path before us and inspiring others to follow!

Filled with the spirit of God, I set off to shine brightly on a path I knew God had prepared for me. A little apprehensive, a little more confident, but entirely determined. I knew that

God had prepared me for the upcoming journey. Every moment leading up to the decision to walk His path was finally what God was preparing for me my entire life.

I want to ask you something. Has God placed something on your heart?

Is there a path you know God needs you to walk?

Do you doubt whether you're prepared for the path ahead?

I encourage you to take the first step.

Ask yourself, how long did it take me to take the first step? Months! It took me months!

Why? Simple, I wanted to do it MY way, not God's! Have you ever felt this way?

I wanted to do it on my terms instead of God's timing! See, I spent my entire life planning every step because all I knew was how to survive, and I didn't know how to be vulnerable for people like me (or people like us). I didn't know how to surrender. So, God, "I said I was ready, and I trust you, but can I walk the path slowly?"

I remember trying to bargain with God, "Lord, I'll walk the path you're asking me to, but can I bubble wrap myself first, reinforced in a blanket so the thorns won't prick me?"

"Our light will shine brighter and brighter, illuminating the path before us and inspiring others to follow!"

irum rashid-jones

Sometimes I would cry, "Lord, I don't want to be hurt! Lord, I don't want to suffer again. But, Lord, can I shine a little from here?"

Have you ever tried to bargain on your terms when God has already cleared and prepared you for the path ahead? "The path of the righteous is like the morning sun, shining ever brighter till the full light of day" in Proverbs 4:18 serves as a reminder to continue walking the lighted path.

When I finally decided to surrender to God, I felt some of my wounds turn into scars overnight. With wounds slowly healing, I felt stronger to bring others to join my journey. One person at a time. To guide, to support, to help shine.

Wisdom Connections:

Ask yourself:

- Why did I spend so many years purposely trying to shrink instead of shining?
- Why did I let past fears serve as my compass through life instead of the light God has placed in us to shine for ourselves or others?
- Who is in the darkness, waiting for you to SHINE your light so they can be pulled out of the dark?
- Who can you save with your light?
- Why would you hide your light instead of allowing it to shine?

I'm asking you today to SHINE. Shine in the Grace or the Glory of God.

Your light is here to help others!

Prayer to God

My prayer and message for you, dear reader… I am praying this over you and want YOU to pray this over your life too!

Dear Lord, I want to let you in as we come to you today with a special prayer. Lord, I pray for your holy presence to be felt today for every woman seeking motivation and encouragement, including myself. Please help us find the courage to take on new challenges and pursue the dreams you've put in our hearts. Please give us the strength to push forward through any adversity that may come our way. Help us never quit on the dream you've put in our hearts.

Remind us at every turn of all we have accomplished this far with your will, strength, and holy power! Help us use those successes as fuel to keep going - when the going gets tough - when we're ready to give up….. Guide us in wise decisions and help us recognize which path will bring us closer to achieving the desired outcomes YOU want us to accomplish!

Help us access the knowledge available to us to equip us with the skills needed to succeed. Instill a sense of determination and perseverance so that we never give up on what matters most. We pray for your wisdom and guidance as we continue this life journey.

Lord, I pray that you shine a path before us so that we always remain strong and confident, filled with courage and determination that brings honor to you! When people look at our actions and success, it is revealed, Lord, it is of YOUR doing! Lord, we pray that the dreams that You put in our hearts and mind become a reality. Lord, we pray that anything we deem challenging in our path creates abundant and prosperous opportunities and that every opportunity we take on leads to more significant successes.

May our hard work pay off in ways that bring joy and satisfaction in our lives and create a life full of peace and happiness for generations ahead. May YOU refill our cup with your hope, faith and joy. Help us live the life we were destined for and that we always feel your Holy presence, love, and Holy power always. Lord, we surrender to YOU. Lord, I surrender to YOU. Amen.

Reflection

wisdom of gratitude

Thanks for Everything!

Lori L. Dixon, Ed.S.

> "Gratitude is a word used to express thankfulness and praise. The Bible teaches us about the power of having a grateful heart. An attitude of thanksgiving has the power to fill us with hope and joy." (Bible Study Tools)

Certain times of the year always bring out gratitude and thanks, such as holidays, birthdays, events, etc. In addition, you may have participated in a "Gratitude challenge" for several days where you thought of and shared thankful thoughts for family, friends, homes, and even pets on social media. My question is, what happens on the day the "gratitude binge and focus" is over? Does our gratefulness change? Does it become about life and work once again? Hopefully not, yet it is a realization and actual occurrence for many people we meet daily.

My mom was a huge follower of Sarah Breathnach when she launched her book "Simple Abundance" and highlighted the journey of gratitude. She always taught us to be incredibly gracious, and my sister was amazingly grateful to everyone. The story I am sharing has always been one of the challenges surrounding my nephew and how his reactions changed how I thought about gratitude forever.

My nephew, Nathaniel, was around three years old when we moved our family to Florida. We had a special bond when I lived near him and his family. For those first few years, we had the opportunity to have him for visits, weekends, and outings, where I could carry him around, pointing out all the wonders of the world, at least "his" world and mine. This included the uniquely formed growing of trees that swayed in the gentle breezes and the flowers of each season with their intricate petal designs and colorful displays in his grandma's yard or mommy's, too. As an aunt with an extraordinary passion for children's literature and the arts, I would be found with him reading tales of animals and imaginary characters, singing silly songs and lullabies, dancing to the rhythm of nature or the song in my head, and painting luscious bright colored swishes across a large piece of paper mounted on an outdoor easel. It was a time of blessings in love, joy, and family. We knew it and treasured every moment.

Probably because of our family's passion for books and reading, I had cultivated an extensive collection fueled by my love affair with any book, especially picture ones filled with colorful images and sensory details. You would find me in a special oversized and stuffed chair with him or on my lap when I could. Even without him checking on the perfect voice and cadence, I would soon share with him sharing the tales of whomever the hero of the story would be. We enjoyed the rhyme and rhythm of Dr. Seuss, the funny adventures of

Bernstein Bears (he loved Daddy Bernstein's voice), and the classics of Good Night, Moon, and The Velveteen Rabbit. Even more importantly, we both treasured those moments of snuggling and listening to adventures and new words to enhance his language and learning together through these books.

My mom, dad, and I moved to Florida when Nathaniel turned three. It was my parent's retirement dream and my goal to attend college there. Little did we know how hard it would be to leave our home, family, friends, life in the Midwest of my own 19 years, and not to mention Nathaniel and my sister. Both were very concerned that when we moved away, we wouldn't be able to read together anymore, spend long weekends and all holidays with each other, and connect as they both needed.

My family and I began brainstorming how we could still be part of their life back in Illinois and bring them into our new life in Florida. Mom and Dad started exploring different beaches and would send pictures, a shell or driftwood, and a tiny bit of sand from each new location. This was before cell phones, Facetime, Zoom, Skype, and all the more recent ways we can now stay a part of each other's daily life. My mom still missed my sister and her grandson desperately. She even began writing her children's book, another story for another day. Yet so did I! I also knew a young child (my degrees were in progress at that time) needed more tangible ways to stay connected with us.

After much creative thought and talking with my sister about what Nathaniel was missing, it came to us like a brick hitting the pavement. Why not ask HIM? Do you know what his response would be? "I miss you being the "Cat in the Hat," "Mr. Berenstain," and what about Lyle in "Lyle, Lyle, Crocodile." How can you not want to jump in your car and drive back to his home and cuddle up with him? Which of course is what he would ask me since young children have no idea where or "who" in Florida?

What did I do? I started by finding, devising, uncovering, and creating a special way to still be there with him and continue to instill the passion for the great literature we had started. At that time, I had a fabulous professor of Children's Literature who knew about my dilemma, so we brought the challenge up to the class I was in with her. The answers and ideas from the students went from flying a private plane to pick him up and reading mid-air to more feasible ones, like reading to other children to practice and then reading to him over the phone.

Yet, the winner that I could envision myself doing and keeping up with was what I felt from the beginning. It was staring me right in the face... my personal tape recorder. It was my VOICE he missed most! Mommy and Daddy could read the same books to him, but not as Auntie Lori could. What did I do? I chose some of our favorite picture books we had already read together and used a tape recorder, yes, and an old piece of technology these days to talk to my nephew as if I was snuggling right next to him. I even called him on the recording to come to cuddle up, which chair to join me in, and let him choose the one we read first, knowing all full well the one it would be. After taping a few stories, I wrapped them all up in a fun way for him to rip through the paper or use a key to open a locked wooden box. I would then place the collection into a shipping box and address it to Nathaniel in the care of my sister. They had so much fun opening it; he would have her play the first one before bed that night.

What was his reaction? I know you are waiting patiently as I was to hear. My sister would always take a picture of him opening the box and capture his expression unveiling it from its container. Then, call me immediately so you can tell me all about his mail delivery. Of course, his very first thought was, "How did Auntie Lori get into the "box" (the tape player) and then it was, "How did you know which stories I would want to read first." You can imagine the joy it gave me to feel like I was there in Nathaniel's room watching it all play out, listening with him, seeing my sister turning those pages ever so slowly with the "beep" I created to turn them just in time to reveal what was next or who was talking now. He repeatedly played those stories and turned those dog-eared pages until he was ready for more to be mailed next month. This became the nightly routine and continued for over two years.

Each month a new set of fresh picture books of exciting adventures, even new characters to learn about, and of course, a cassette tape with my voice sharing why I chose that book just for him and now asking questions about his thoughts and predictions, too. Yes, we both grew together in our love for books, which cushioned the feelings of being unable to get together in person. Even with my ever-changing life in Florida and his gains in age, book interests, and focus, these packages continued to arrive. Did he put aside and forget about the previous ones? Of course not. They remained in his bedroom to listen to Aunt Lori talk and read long after he could read them for himself. I wanted these packages to be more than just my voice and some books. I focused on making them filled with laughter, stories of what I was doing with Grandma and Grandpa that day, funny things in Florida, and even a few sounds of the beach in the background, which he loved dearly. These gifts were filled with our lives and our lives, which still included him.

Yes, my sister, my brother-in-law sometimes, and my nephew would come and visit, or we would go and see them, too. Yet, nothing did we do that kept us going during the lulls of these infrequent visits than those tapes and books.

My nephew would get on the phone monthly for at least three years and say thank you. Then, when things changed, I heard the silly laughter and conversations around his gratitude for which book or story did, he love the most to a struggle even at my sister's prompting to talk with grandma or me. I knew it wasn't necessary to him in his life as it once was when his gratitude shifted drastically to a statement of … "Thank you for everything, Aunt Lori, love you, BYE," and he would run off to play or move on to other things in their busy day. There was no talking about his preschool life, new friends, or view of the world as it was changing, no… "tell me what YOU are doing, Aunt Lori" anymore.

That became the precedent. Even though I knew how very much he loved each book and tape in my "heartfelt" boxes, the response still wasn't what we once shared. I would even prompt him, or my sister would ask, "Which story did you like the most?" and "Didn't you think it was funny about Grandma and Grandpa?"

Unfortunately, this became the norm as he grew from preschool to elementary. Other packages with favorite items for holidays and birthdays or for "just because" moments gleaned the same quick response, "thanks for everything, love you, BYE." My reaction would be the same "But what about…" Our relationship changed. Those grateful opportunities became fewer and fewer, and the closeness we once had slipped away. I did understand mentally, yet my heart was missing the feedback and conversations we once had. It wasn't that I didn't want him to grow up or that I was upset that he didn't acknowledge me in his life anymore. It was the way he gave back by being grateful. It struck me as odd since my sister was so aware of the importance of being thankful and was the BEST gift giver. She would send something to my parents or me just because she thought we would like it. My sister Susie was the same way with her children and her friends. Susie tried desperately to infuse that into her son, but it didn't take hold and grow.

Thankfulness is an asset we feel we should instill in our children, yet we often find that the importance grows and needs to be cultivated again in adulthood. Over the years of my practice, I have created strategies to enhance thank you moments into a memorable, easy, and structured way to use and model in writing or even verbally. There are three questions to include in your gratitude:

1. What are you thankful or thanking the person for?
2. How did their kindness or strengths and assets impact you personally?
3. How did their kindness or sharing of those assets make you feel?

Can you see how Nathaniel could have used this structure to create even more connection and communication between us using gratitude? What would it look like? He could say, "I am thankful you made this for me, Aunt Lori. The one book, …, is my favorite this time. I love hearing your voice; the funny voices make me feel like you are still here. Whenever I read the books you send and hear you talk about Florida, I feel loved by you." You can imagine how Nathaniel and I would have felt more connected through our little packages.

Can you think of an opportunity to use this structure? What answers would you have, and to whom? Thankfulness and gratitude are assets that everyone must have to be successful in life, especially in relationships.

> "Gratitude unlocks the fullness of life. It turns what we have into enough and more. It turns denial into acceptance, chaos into order, and confusion into clarity. It can turn a meal into a feast, a house into a home, a stranger into a friend."
> —Melody Beattie

When I was working with another author, she included this concept and its power in life and even the workplace. She loved using fun phrases, memorable quotes, and inspirational images. Her work and research showed that sometimes it's not just ordinary gratitude you need to use but a stronger impact on that person by (her phrasing) "knocking their socks off." In the quality research by William Glasser, he shares that going "above and beyond" is the highest and most important form of quality. Who would you want to "knock their socks off"? When we design and execute a plan of action, we will receive an overwhelming feeling of joy in return.

> "Always give thanks to Father God for every person (for all people) he brings into your life in the name of our Lord Jesus Christ." Ephesians 5:20 The Passion Translation

The Greek text of the above scripture relates to how we give thanks not only to every person but to all people and to give thanks for all things. How powerful are those words!? If we realize that the action of gratitude is a pathway to praise for our Father God, we can see how praising him in his creation, in his influence, in his work in us, and in all things that matter to us. Wow!

Walking with the Lord isn't measured by how grateful you are.

Today, many opportunities exist to say thank you with a genuine reason and purpose. It becomes a way to connect with others to impact and influence rather than just being transactional. For instance, we know our pharmacists, dry cleaners, baristas of the local coffee shop, and store owners in our community. We call them by name, thank them, ask how they are, and bring them our business and referrals. You can begin the routine of thanking teachers, staff, administrators, bus drivers, cafeteria workers, UPS and FedEx drivers and clerks, the cashier at a store you shop, service men and women, and even our friends and family. Choose an "off" time from a holiday that negates the true gratefulness impact. Make it a random part of your day.

" Walking with the Lord isn't measured by how grateful you are."

Lori L. dixon

Take moments to say how much you appreciate them and why when you have the chance. It will help us change how people see their lives and those of others. Modeling this level of gratitude affects everyone around you. For example, we bring our grandchildren where we go. They are impacted by those standing in line with us to see how to care for others we encounter daily—focusing on a thank you for those who appear to be doing you a service when they may never be thanked for the job they do every day.

What happened to my nephew, Nathaniel? Did his gratitude and thankfulness become important as he grew up? No, unfortunately. I wish I could say he began seeing life more abundantly or treating others with respect and honor. But, unfortunately, that would not be true. I hope one day he will.

My mission is to shift how others SEE those around them and find ways to bring love and compassion into their lives, even for a moment. I DO it for Nathaniel. I DO it for those who didn't learn gratitude in their own life… YET.

I ask you to find new ways to enhance Gratitude and Thankfulness in your life to celebrate God's breathtaking and personal creation for YOU. Will you begin with a journal? There are reflection pages just for you in this chapter. So start a practice now and praise…be joyful, sing, dance, and share it with others.

> "Let JOY be your continual feast. Make your life a prayer. And in everything, always give thanks, for this is God's perfect plan for YOU in Christ Jesus." 1 Thessalonians 5:18 The Passion Translation

What about a prayer of gratitude? I am providing one for you today from a dear friend who wrote this. Thank you, Katrina, for your "thanks-filled" heart and compassionate wisdom for others to remind us of the many things we must be grateful for.

Prayer to God

Thank you, God
Thank you for this day
Thank you for the air I breathe
Thank you for the gift of life

Thank you, God
Thank you for my bed
Thank you for my shower
Thank you for the roof over my head
Thank you for my home
Thank you for warmth
Thank you for my healthy body
Thank you for the earth beneath my feet
Thank you for my freedom

Thank you, God
Thank you for this day
Thank you for the air I breathe
Thank you for the gift of life

Thank you, God
Thank you for my intuition
Thank you for travel
Thank you for my ability to replenish and rejuvenate
Thank you for companionship
Thank you for the plants
Thank you for my ability to visualize

Thank you for the flowers
Thank you for my ability to dream
Thank you for the trees
Thank you for my ability to co-create with you all my desires

Thank you, God
Thank you for this day
Thank you for the air I breathe
Thank you for the gift of life

Thank you, God
Thank you for the sun
Thank you for my ability to create wealth
Thank you for the moon
Thank you for my ability to do what I love
Thank you for the wind
Thank you for reflection
Thank you for all my teachers
Thank you for my creativity
Thank you for my capacity to feel joy
Thank you for light
Thank you for sound
Thank you for my playfulness
Thank you for my ability to have wholesome, loving relationships
Thank you for laughter
Thank you for rest

Thank you, God
Thank you for this day
Thank you for the air I breathe
Thank you for the gift of life

Thank you, God
Thank you for delicious foods and drinks

Thank you for my ability to touch and be touched
Thank you for the beauty of nature
Thank you for my ability to forgive
Thank you for all the seasons
Thank you for my ability to heal
Thank you for wildlife
Thank you for my ability to achieve financial freedom
Thank you for my passions

Thank you, God
Thank you for this day
Thank you for the air I breathe
Thank you for the gift of life

Thank you, God
Thank you for my strong bones
Thank you for my strong muscles
Thank you for my healthy heart
Thank you for my strong back
Thank you for my legs
Thank you for my feet
Thank you for my arms
Thank you for my hands
Thank you for my eyes
Thank you for my ears
Thank you for my taste buds
Thank you for my healthy digestive system
Thank you for my balanced nervous system

Thank you for the night sky
Thank you for all my lessons
Thank you for the stars

Thank you, God

Thank you for this day
Thank you for the air I breathe
Thank you for the gift of life

Thank you, God
Thank you for the oceans and the seas
Thank you for silence
Thank you for the forests
Thank you for my self-respect
Thank you for the mountains
Thank you for my ability to feel inner peace
Thank you for the rain
Thank you for my ability to sleep peacefully
Thank you for the infinite opportunities available to me
Thank you for all my senses

Thank you, God
Thank you for this day
Thank you for the air I breathe
Thank you for the gift of life

Thank you, God
Thank you for water
Thank you for fresh fruits and vegetables
Thank you for my ability to live with authenticity
Thank you for choice
Thank you for the balance of life
Thank you for transportation
Thank you for my capacity to unconditionally self-love
Thank you for my family
Thank you for my friends
Thank you for compassion

Than

k you, God
Thank you for this day
Thank you for the air I breathe
Thank you for the gift of life

Thank you, God
Thank you for kindness
Thank you for my ability to give and receive.

Thank you, God
Thank you for this day
Thank you for the air I breathe
Thank you for the gift of life

Thank you, God
Thank you for the process of realizing my innate perfection in you
Thank you for movement
Thank you for my ability to learn and grow
Thank you for new beginnings
Thank you for my ability to have a deep, fulfilling, romantic relationship
Thank you for color
Thank you for my ability to make peace with my body
Thank you for music
Thank you for my ability to trust
Thank you for books
Thank you for my inner sanctuary

Thank you, God
Thank you for this day
Thank you for the air I breathe
Thank you for the gift of life

Thank you, God
Thank you for dance

Thank you for my natural talents
Thank you for my vibrant energy
Thank you for my inner wisdom
Thank you for my healthy boundaries
Thank you for all my experiences
Thank you for all my blessings
Thank you for my capacity to love and be loved
Thank you for my unique spark of the divine within
Thank you for my connection to all that is

Thank you, God
Thank you for this day
Thank you for the air I breathe
Thank you for the gift of life

Amen

Reflection

let joy be your continual feast

1 Thessalonians 5:18

intentional connections

Moms and Daughters

Allison Byrd-Haley

"I have no greater joy than to hear that my children are walking in the truth." 3 John 1:4

In my life experiences, two words only make sense when paired: *mother* and *daughter.* I am not thinking about expression or cliché but more about how mothers and daughters are connected throughout their lives. The connection between my mother and me remains incomparable due to a mutual outpouring of selfless love, affirmation, and understanding. My mother parented us with an "all-in" philosophy that I didn't begin to understand until I became a mother myself. Mom took her role as a mother seriously, always making herself available. Mom enjoyed every aspect of motherhood. Even when parenting was unpleasant, Mom cheerfully continued because she had signed up for the whole package.

In August 1975, when Mom went into labor with me, she sat in a theater watching the movie *JAWS*. I mention this because of an anecdote my mother enjoyed sharing about my birth. Because I was breech and she pushed me out rear-end-first, my mother would chuckle when she sometimes pondered if the doctors should have used the jaws of life for my delivery. Of course, given the decades of medical advancements since, cesarean sections have become the standard if the baby is breech and the doctor cannot easily turn the baby. Mom didn't have that option, but what a champ I had for a mother! I have always marveled at her strength and thank God that her example also molded me into a fighter. Before going any further, though, it is imperative to add that even though my story is about mothers and daughters, I feel incredibly blessed with the fantastic father and sons God has given me!

Before the birth of my sister and me, my mother suffered two miscarriages. As heartbreaking as those must have been, she needed to put her pain and fear aside and cling to God to see her hopes of raising a family realized. Within the next few years, my mother had two healthy daughters to raise. I'm not sure she ever thought about how her unconditional love and desire for motherhood would touch and affect the next generation, her grandchildren. Looking back, I am so grateful for how she sacrificed her time; took moments and made them teachable; paid attention to influences around us; was our constant encouragement, and was in our corner.

Of course, as an adult now, I understand the daily energy and consistency that is needed to be an effective parent. Double that when a child has a mental health diagnosis. For example, at age three, I was diagnosed with ADHD. I can fully appreciate all of this because my oldest daughter received the same diagnosis. Mom used to say that when I was a child, I would walk across the street to the other side and *only then* think to look both ways. She said I did this even while holding her hand. My impulsivity and constant movement certainly sharpened my mother's vigilance and physical fitness, having to keep up with me during those early years.

For many reasons, I viewed my mother as a superhero. She was made up of so many good things rolled into one; she was loving, kind, unselfish, and highly watchful of us kids. In retrospect, I know she parented this way for our safety. It's likely, too, that it stemmed from her recurring fear that someone might snatch her child if she looked away. I seem to remember that some of the top stories in the news in those days involved the kidnappings of children.

Nevertheless, as some of my friends of the same age began experiencing slightly less parental oversight, my mom wouldn't buy in. So, despite Mom's excellent qualities, I didn't appreciate or like any of her over-protectiveness in grade school. I thought it stunk!

One thing that bothered me was that I could not ride my bike or walk to school even though we only lived two blocks away. Of course, I regularly made pleading attempts to change her mind. I tried my hardest; I promised and begged. "Please, Mom! I *promise* I will stay close to my friends!" Though with every best effort from me, Mom lovingly came back with a firm, "No." Like all moms, I'm sure mine wanted us to be safe. At any rate, Mom was always thinking far ahead of me, knowing my impulsiveness could be to my detriment. She was intentional in that way and always on alert.

Unquestionably, Mom kept a constant eye on us kids. She did not regularly send us to the neighbors' houses to play to free up some time for herself. She was happiest when she was with us. At around age six, one of my earliest memories is begging my parents to allow me to become a Brownie Scout. Receiving permission was not the issue. The problem was that the Troop I wanted to join for my area had recently lost its leader. So, my mother stepped up when all my friends' parents got together, and none of the other mothers came forward to fill the position. If she hadn't, we wouldn't have been able to have a Brownie Troop, and I probably never would have been a Brownie.

With that in mind, when I think about what my mother did in her spare time, I can't remember her ever having any. Her free time was devoted to her kids. As an adult, I more fully appreciate the many sacrifices she made. I have often wondered and sometimes feel sad that maybe Mom missed out on pursuing other paths in her life. Occasionally, Mom mentioned she had an interest in nursing. On the other hand, she could have pursued a degree while still raising her kids. I know my mother would have been fantastic at both because she could juggle many things at once, was brilliant, and treated everyone like a family member.

Even on the hard days or when I pushed her buttons, Mom continued to express her love. My mother's love was unwavering, and I am so grateful to have experienced this from her. It is hard for me to understand how not every child receives this from a parent. My mother always told us she loved us whether the day was good or bad. For as long as I can remember, Mom would say, "I love you more!" Today, this saying hangs in my office to encourage me. Other than *telling me* she loved me, she *showed* it daily through her actions. I remember when I was ten and broke my leg by colliding with a car on my bicycle. Mom probably told me a thousand times before never to ride my bike in the alley, yet that day I did. The crash happened when I accidentally rode my bike into a moving vehicle. Instead of my mom reprimanding me or showing her disappointment, my mother's loving heart cared for me throughout six months of wearing a cast and physical therapy.

I could share so many instances from my childhood that are just the most delightful memories illustrating the kind of

Mom she was. I cherish moments due to their sweet and simple nature showing a mom who was always present, coming to my rescue, and having the house where all my friends wanted to hang out. My Mom was considered "the caring mom" who tried to provide experiences for us kids that would afford us happy memories and make the most of our childhood years.

As I entered adolescence, I learned that Mom was growing weary about some changes in Plano, Texas, and, to make it worse, I was about to enter junior high school. Plano had become a popular, growing suburb. With the influx of people, Plano was becoming crowded. In Mom's opinion, with the rapidly growing population, the common traditional values shared among residents were fading and being replaced by materialism. As a result, Mom wanted us to move from Plano and return to a simpler life in the country. So, when I was around thirteen, my Mom found a beautiful house about thirty miles away, and our family moved to Rowlett, Texas.

Life in Rowlett was different. For my sister and me, it was a culture shock. At the time, Rowlett was an outlying community primarily made of farmland and pastures. The population was relatively small back then compared to Plano. Moving only a short distance from Plano, I was surprised to hear all the kids my age speaking with country accents. Even though we had a beautiful house, we only lived there for a year when the family moved to nearby Mesquite, Texas. This was short-lived because my father got transferred to work in the Chicago area where my dad grew up, and his family still lived. This would be an exciting opportunity where I could get to know his side of the family better. Until then, my only interactions with them occurred during our trips to Chicago every summer to visit. I always had fun with my family and imagined living near them would be a blast! Mom, however, seemed to have reservations about the idea. So, I made a list of all the positives and approached my mother. I vividly recall the chair she sat in that day as I gave her my best sales pitch, hoping to persuade her. It worked! Mom wanted what her daughters wanted, so we went off to Chicago.

My Italian grandmother graciously invited us to move in so my parents could have more time to find a place to live. It didn't take long, though, for things to start unraveling. In a relatively short time, my fifteen-year-old self-learned that there is a difference between vacationing with and visiting family versus the reality of daily living. All the "fun" I had hoped for never materialized. I hadn't considered that people have things to do in their lives that I didn't see during our summer visits. Adding to the disappointment, it became evident daily that my mom was unhappy in Chicago. Mom was usually content everywhere, so it needed to be clarified. I also hadn't considered how moving away from *her* family in Texas would affect my mother. To make a move, Mom sacrificed living near her mother, sister, and friends. She also left behind a job she had enjoyed for over ten years.

We moved back to Plano six months later due to my mom's unhappiness. Our time in Chicago came to an end. It was sad to leave our family, but at the time, we decided it was best. While my dad stayed on to fulfill a full year of employment at his job, Mom, my sister, and I moved into an apartment in Plano until my father returned. I remember how much my mother did not like living in the apartment. However, my sister and I loved it because it was across the street from the mall! We spent a LOT of time there while my dad was in Chicago. With him not around, we also made the most of testing the limits with my mom, especially me. Disagreements between us increased. One minute she was the best mother on earth. The next minute she was the worst, and we would argue about how she was unreasonable and completely unfair. I was sure I had no part to play in these arguments (wink… yeah, right).

When Dad finished his work in Chicago, he rejoined us in Texas, and we moved into what became their final home purchase with children under the same roof. Mom and Dad quickly transformed the house into a home, and my sister and I were happy! Now in the middle years of my teens and wanting to act like one, I didn't want any rules to hold me back. I thought life without restrictions would be incredible.

As my teen years went on, my anxiety got worse. Finally, my mother and I reached a point where we recognized it wasn't healthy or normal. I needed outside help to address the cause and learn practical strategies to reduce it. My issues and anxiety had grown to a point where they adversely affected my overall well-being. Yet, in all her compassion, Mom attended the sessions with me for support.

Perhaps one of the most challenging years for my mother as a parent was watching me get engaged at age 18. My Mom instinctively knew from the start that my husband-to-be was not a good match for her daughter. However, none of that mattered to me at the time. He and I had plans, the first of which started that summer when we moved to California near his family. Secretly marrying right before we left, we packed the car and started our drive. Not long into the drive, I began to feel sick. I reasoned that maybe I had carsickness. As we continued to drive, I couldn't keep anything in my stomach, so we had to make frequent stops so I could puke on the side of the road. A few times, with nowhere to pull off, the best I had was rolling down the window. It was awful.

As you may have already guessed—unknown to me at the time—I was in my first weeks of pregnancy. To no one's surprise, things didn't go as planned in California. Within a month, we packed the car again and returned to Texas. Along the way, I saw flashing neon signs telling me my marriage was in trouble. The man I had married was into drugs and abusive, and I wanted no part of it. After we returned to Texas, he and I lived apart.

At one of my doctor appointments during my pregnancy, I discovered I was having a girl. On that same day, my maternal grandmother passed away. I firmly believe that God controls everything, including correlations that He designs and places before us. Some people take notice and refer to them as coincidences. I view these connections as "God-winks," intentionally sent to us as messages of hope and comfort to signal that He is real. God-winks assure us of life beyond this earth. This unique and special association of life and death between my unborn daughter and grandmother permanently united my mom with my baby that day. Learning that I was carrying her granddaughter filled my mom with immeasurable hope during a mourning period following her mother's passing.

Then about three months before I turned nineteen, Katerina "Katie" Marie was born. I chose the middle name Marie because the first three letters matched the first three of my mother's name, Marilyn. During the hours at the hospital before delivery, Mom was with me. When I was told I could have one person with me during my epidural placement, I chose my mom without hesitation. Mom was present for the births of all her grandchildren. To her, these moments were among her most cherished. Upon the delivery of Katie, Mom added a new role and name to her life. Mom was now a grandmother, and her grandchildren would call her "Mimi."

I remember the nurse placing her on my chest after Katie was born. What I felt in that moment is beyond words, even today. This beautiful baby was all mine. Before any reality of "Now what do I do?" and "How do I do it?" crossed my mind, my mom was beside me, affirming that I would make a fantastic mother. She didn't remind me of my age or anything working against me. Instead, she filled the room with optimism and assurance for Katie's and my future.

During my first month at home in my apartment with baby Katie, Mom came over every morning to help me. She provided it no matter what was needed: feeding Katie, doing laundry, and cleaning. I also gave my marriage another try but soon decided that I wanted more for Katie's future. Plus, mine. I chose to leave her biological father and never looked back. Fortunately, I had a lot of emotional support, so I knew things would be okay. There were also periods when Mom stepped forward to continue parenting me with her intentional style. After all, I was only nineteen. Looking back on the perspectives of both mother and daughter, I understand this completely. I immensely enjoyed those first years with Katie, where we learned, laughed, and grew together.

A few years after Katie's arrival, I remarried and soon gave birth to a son, Troy. Unfortunately, my sweet baby boy entered the world with several health issues from day one. One problem led to another, until approximately fifteen months later, Troy was diagnosed with retinoblastoma (cancer of the eye). Mom was my rock while I focused most of my time on him. He and I were inseparable. I took him to his doctor's appointments and stayed by his side. Though it was unfair to Katie to spend so much time apart, I felt that Troy needed me more. I had to focus on him, his care, and his comfort.

Back then, I didn't have the wisdom to explain things to my young daughter. Because of her age, I felt that sharing so many adult things with her could frighten and rob her of her innocence. As it was, little Katie had a lot to handle due to her developing strong-willed spirit. After Troy was born, I didn't notice that our mother-and-daughter relationship shifted. Some might say that I took my time with Katie for granted, but in my defense, I had a medically fragile newborn who needed his mom's full attention. I regret that I didn't carve out time for her and me.

Overall, we survived the few years of Troy's medical treatments, and by the grace of God, he was cancer-free. Unfortunately, things didn't work out with Troy's dad and me, so I was again a single mom with two bright and spirited children. However, I felt like I could finally catch my breath after enduring many years filled with overflowing stress from Troy's cancer.

Katie was determined to push limits during her adolescent years. She sought freedom from restrictions just as I had at her age. Admittedly, at times, I could have handled things better. My style of intentional parenting could have been a lot better. Thank goodness my mom was there to support my small family and me as I continued to "grow" my purposeful ways of communicating and interacting.

During these years, I met and married the man Katie considers her "dad." Along with marrying him, God blessed me with three bonus children, Samantha, Shayne, and Christian. So grateful for two more sons, but I loved having another daughter. It was a bonus! I have a special bond with both of my daughters. We each have the same tattoo that is special to us. Katie and I have a tattoo that means eternal. I mentioned that because I talked about eternal love at my mom's funeral. That comes from the last piece of jewelry from my mom to Katie and me. The tattoo my youngest daughter and I have are angel wings. I call her my angel due to God knew I needed her in my life.

One of the most challenging moments of Katie's life occurred at age seventeen when my mom, Mimi, was diagnosed with advanced cancer. I can still feel the devastation and shock I experienced the day I was told. I went into action mode and tried to find any doctor that could perform a miracle! Katie stepped up to also care for Mimi. Unfortunately, Mom's cancer was too advanced, and she left us after three months of diagnosis. Mom's death came much too quickly. Why did we not have more time?

Though we are physically separated from my mom now, I can feel her around me daily. So when we leave this place, we will take the love to heaven. Remember handsome Patrick Swayze? That sweet soul passed from cancer too. Well, he was in this film… you may have heard of it. GHOST! That was my mom's favorite movie. He told the love of his life that he was taking the love with him. So I believe my mom will be there with all her love to give when I get to heaven.

Katie and I recently took a much-needed vacation to Florida and had a wonderful time at Disney as mother and daughter. We thoroughly enjoyed moments of fun and happiness. I cherished that time with my incredible daughter!

I founded *Heavenly Mimi* in honor of my

"No matter how many hard times we muddle through or how many tears we shed, our bond always connects us."

allison byrd-haley

mother, who lived her life making a difference for others. *Heavenly Mimi* continues Mom's walk by selflessly assisting people with cancer. I understand the financial hardships associated with cancer treatments from first-hand experience. Mom taught me by example; continuing her legacy is my heart's desire and calling. Providing relief and blessings for others is our honor, and it connects Katie and me in the sweetest ways. Serving others together has brought us closer as our wounds continue to heal. My mom would always say, "I will be there." That is what I want to do every day with everyone I encounter.

My mother always told me that having children was one of her greatest joys. This is also my joy, no matter how many hard times we muddle through or how many tears we shed. Our bond always connects us. I cherish being a mother and a daughter today and every day. I pray that you find closeness with your generational connections, as well.

Prayer to God

Thank you for mothers.

Thank you for daughters.

Thank you for creating the bond between these two dynamic types of individuals who can create unconditional love between them.

Thank you for giving us opportunities to fail at parenting and to learn to follow how intentional you planned it to be in our lives.

We know how important family is in God's kingdom, and we pray for guidance in how to become the intention of it evident on this earth.

Thank you for showing us how the gift of your Father's love can bring us to see this within our families today.

Amen.

Reflection

I have no greater joy than to hear that my children are walking in the truth.

3 John 1:4

wisdom of family

Yours, Mine, and Ours

Lori L. Dixon, Ed.S.

"For this reason, I kneel before the Father, from whom his whole family (fatherhood, Father's name) in heaven and on earth derives its name." Ephesians 3:15 NIV

"So I kneel humbly before in awe before the Father of our Lord Jesus, the Messiah, the perfect Father of every Father and child in heaven and on earth." Ephesians 3:15 The Passion Translation

We have all been raised on the meaning of "family" in our lives. Whether that means dad, mom, sister, brother, baby, OR if it was mom, stepdad, half-sister, full brother, and you, it is all still family.

For me, the family has always been a challenging concept. Why? Did I have one? Yes! Yet mine may have been very different than yours. My ideas around family have gone through many new and unique meanings and changes as I get older. Let me explain further.

At 11 days old, my biological parents took me to a foster care home with a caregiver who was a nurse. My health challenges at birth required me to be taken care of by her while I awaited a family. A young couple received a phone call from a special agency and had two visits scheduled with different foster homes, one with an infant boy and another with an infant girl. They walked into a small house with a tiny infant sleeping soundly. The man scooped her up gently. The baby girl fit into his outstretched hand and opened her big blue eyes to look into his loving face. Then, as he smiled back at her, he turned and said to the woman, "She is so dinky small, and I think she's OURS!" The woman held her next and cradled her close to her shoulder, "I think she IS ours," she whispered as the little girl fell back soundly to sleep. The man and woman said to the nurse, "We will take her home with us." The caregiver nodded with a smile. She gathered the few baby items up and gave them to the man. Once in the car, the man said, "We don't need to see the little boy now, do we?" The woman smiled broadly, laughed, and shook her red-haired head "no" as they drove away, ready to start a new adventure together as a family. Once they walked in the door, my sister squealed with delight since she had been praying for a baby sister since she was little. Now, their family was complete… wait a minute… I mean, MY family was complete. Hadn't I been looking and waiting, too? No one ever asked me how I felt about it. That will be a discussion as we walk a little further.

You may be asking, "What just happened?" Yes, I AM ADOPTED! It was a journey to be chosen as an infant to become part of an extraordinary family. Yet, there is more to the story, as you can imagine. Everyone I knew in school, church, neighborhood, and even my friend circle had questions. My "new" mom was excited to share the story with anyone who would listen, and yes, they told me... over and over and over again. Some children don't know they are adopted, some families choose to share it later in life with them, and some, like my family, share every detail, especially the part about how LOVED I was. Unfortunately, not every other child out there was kind about it while I was growing up. Some bullied me and made my adoption seem more like abandonment by my first mother and family. Yes, children can be cruel, as we know.

When kids made those comments in my early years, I cried to my mom because I had not yet established a response to these mean-spirited children. But my mom was a quick wit and could make you laugh, so her canned comment and rebuttal were hysterical, and I learned to say it well. "That may be true that my first mom didn't hold on to me, but my next. Mom DID. My parents also CHOSE me... your parents HAD to take YOU home." Wow! Can you imagine their faces and the conversation with their family when they ran into the house? I remember it well and still chuckle.

God brings us into this world exactly when He wants us here with the families He has envisioned to "train us up" through His words and promises. We are learning to fulfill our mission, assignment, and purpose for furthering His Kingdom on Earth. Does this mean that "man" gets in the way of this sometimes and isn't fully walking in His purpose for them? Yes, there is free will, and the enemy sometimes gets in the way of derailing this path.

We have heard Proverbs 22:6 tell us, "Train up a child in the way he should go; even when he is old, he will not depart from it." This scripture is for parents and extended family, too. In many churches, they dedicate young children to God. The parents and entire family agree to bring their child in the ways provided by the Word. They promise to be aligned, and the supportive family members, including the church community, agree to be there as the parents take the "oath" of this walk of faith.

> "No family design is perfect. It is only closer to perfect when God is at the center, guiding us."
>
> *lori l. dixon*

Family brings forth and nurtures children as they learn and walk in their individual and combined purpose for God. No family is perfect. No family design is perfect. It is only closer to perfect when God is at the center, guiding us.

Even though different, our family design was led by God and directed by my mom, dad, and my sister, Susie. When I was young, adoption wasn't as prevalent as now. However, I vividly remember in middle school when my teacher asked me to speak to her classes about what was to be adopted and let them ask questions. Wow, what 13-year-old wants to stand up to 30 peers and tell them about their birth? Me! It was fun to talk about something meaningful to me and a story I had heard 1,000 times around my birth. As an adult, I can still hear my mom telling it to me and how she talked, her inflection, the emotion she exuded, and how she told the story to anyone that asked.

Families come in all shapes and sizes, even more so now. Adoption has become a household name and not as unusual. However, adopting a "new" family structure challenges many adopted children. Feeling "part" of the family is all part of what age the child was adopted, how other children will adjust and react, and the rest of the extended family's reactions. Yet, knowing where they came from, their birth story, and why they were "given up" for adoption is sometimes shared with the child; other times, there is no information.

I was blessed to be in a family that loved me dearly. Being raised in a strong Christian family and having opportunities to flourish was precisely what God needed me to have then. I never wondered about my story on the other side of adoption until others asked. It made me feel that there was more to my life that I didn't know. Even teachers could be cruel in their lack of understanding with me.

For instance, one teacher in middle school assigned us the homework of designing and learning about our family "tree." We had to draw and create it and put factual information about family, generations, and any interesting legacies they were leaving behind for us. So Mom and Dad sat down with me, and we began crafting the genealogy of our tree for both sides. I LOVED art projects and saw I was drawing a tree and what others had planted for us to learn from and grow. He had a wonderful time doing this as a family. He laughed about silly stories involving Grandpa or Grandma and giggled over the names of great-grandparents and even their parents, like Valentious Green and many others. These moments bonded us further and deeper into realizing ancestry roots. But that was about to become undone.

Doubt is always the work of the enemy in us. Doubt leads us to fear, and fear of our identity or worth is a deep wound when we are young. The teacher assigned my amazingly creative family project didn't plan on what mine would reveal. My family didn't fathom what my teacher's reaction would be, either. I was smiling inside and out as I carried my family "tree" into the classroom, ready to present it in detail, creativity, artistic expression, and generational mapping. I couldn't wait to present it in front of the whole class. The anticipation was palpable, and my heart was racing with excitement. I wasn't nervous about presenting since I had been singing and speaking in front of groups and our church my whole life. It was anticipation and a little pride around what I had learned. I sat there watching others and how they shared about family structure, grandparents, great-grandparents, aunts and uncles, and some even shared their pets. How fun! Our teacher smiled, nodded, commented, and wrote notes about our presentations. She called my name next. I nearly jumped out of my desk chair to get up to the front of the class. I felt prepared, but was I ready for what happened next? No. As I walked through the design and the structure of my "tree," my classmates listened, smiled, and laughed with me at the funny names and the history of Denmark, Ireland, and England in my grandparents' journey to America. I was honored to share their roots and their past.

When I finished, the students clapped as we all did for each other. My teacher smiled and finished writing on her evaluation paper that I would receive at the end of the class period. I couldn't wait to see the teacher's comments and grade on my special project. We each filed to the teacher's desk and picked up our paper on the way to the next class. I, too, grabbed mine in anticipation. What? A "D"? I was shocked and deeply hurt! Didn't the teacher understand the intricacies of this project, the hard work we put in, the creative design, and my heart shared? Obviously not. The comments were strange, too. "This is an amazing project; you can see your work on its overall image and deep historical connection. Yet, you didn't complete the assignment. This is your family tree, not your adoptive parents' tree. You needed to research YOUR roots and share them with us."

This hurt me deeply. Her words of ignorance cut into my heart. I sat in the next class, thank goodness, at the end of the day, waiting for the bell to ring so I could go home. Mom was picking me up because I carried the project and to hear about how well it was received. When I crawled into the car, Mom knew something was wrong. She pulled the car over into the parking lot across the street. She took a deep breath and asked me, "What happened... I've not seen you this way before?" All I could do was burst into tears and hand her the paper from my teacher. My mom read the comments and saw the words that discredited my work. What came next was a bit of a blur. Mom turned that car around and parked at the school's front door. She and I exited the car and marched into the front office. Mom said she needed to see the principal, and he came out.

All I remember is going into his office, my teacher being called to the impromptu meeting, and a loud discussion occurring. You can imagine how angry my mom was and how eloquently she shared my project accuracy for MY FAMILY. There was no other family in my life. The principal was shocked at the actions and words of the teacher! The teacher apologized greatly for her mistake and said she would change the grade for an amazingly creative and well-thought-out project. The grade was changed from "D" to "A+," and we walked out of the glass doors. Mom with a giant smile on her face for doing battle on my behalf, and me a small smile for the new grade reflecting the work.

Why a slight smile? As you can see, this memory is ingrained in my heart. My mom handled the grade and helped the teacher better understand adoption and adopted children. Yet, the event was still there for me. The humiliation in the classroom of my friends seeing my grade was secondary. The "wound" was re-opened from the times people said my "mom" didn't want me and I was "given away." The wound was there for a young girl in the most critical time of emotional development and identity creation.

Adopted children may feel the "wounds" of abandonment, lack of identity, or a sense of being unworthy. My adopted mom's unresolved fear and sense of worth sometimes was a challenge to overcome the reactions in my own life around my adoption, too. I carried my wounds and hers. It became a way of operating in life for me. I felt responsible for others' feelings and thoughts. Later in life, my mom and I worked through forgiveness and love with each other.

My faith and constant search for approval and community with others who accepted me just like I was, adopted, abandoned, chosen, or alone didn't matter to God. God became my consistent companion in life. Mom and Dad used to laugh that I was like Jesus in the way I was always at the church and the last one to leave. What they didn't know is I belonged there. I was accepted there for the me I wanted to share with everyone. I studied, asked questions, attended, and grew up in my faith. My wounds were lessened there, and I gave my life to Christ at ten years old because he was healing me. Later, I received the Holy Spirit, but that's a different story.

I was raised with my mom's favorite scripture, no matter the adversity. Yes, there were many for me, health, relationships, family, loss, and like many others, we may choose to rise and hold on to the Holy Spirit's compassion and guidance or falter in our faith in pain. It was always a choice in my home.

> "I can do ALL things in Him (Christ) who gives me strength."
> Philippians 4:13 NIV

Yet, recently, I have read and clung to the same scripture in Philippians 4:12-13 of the Passion Translation, "I know what it means to lack, and I know what it means to experience overwhelming abundance, for I'm trained in the secret of overcoming things, whether in fullness or hunger. And I find that the strength of Christ's explosive power infuses me to conquer every difficulty." Wow! Feel it, hear it at your core, and digest it into your body to allow it to feed you.

My parents supported me and realized that some of my struggles taught me to rely on others when in need. There were times, though, just like many of you, I didn't receive the understanding or the acceptance I craved. My dad was always there to guide me, counsel me, and give me a picture of what unconditional love looked like. My mom was slightly different. She loved me dearly, yet, there was a bar I needed to reach for an outward showing of that love. Later in life, we talked through so many things, and I am blessed to have been with her as she approached her "move to Heaven."

You still may wonder. Even with the love of my family, there was a wound of needing to feel loved and accepted. After my dad's early and unexpected passing, my mom received a phone call from a young woman looking for me. Was it a shock? Yes. Did my mom's assurance of having me in her life waver? Definitely. But… God created this special touch on my life. I just had to do it while honoring my mom's wishes.

Here's how God works! After my father's death and my struggle even further with my feeling of being accepted and loved, God wanted me to know my birth story! I was married and only 24 years old. Yet, He made it possible through that phone call, and only after an hour of hearing about my birth, my birth mom, and my family did I begin to feel whole. The connection to my birth sister was profound. I thought about her many times after that and wondered if, later in my life, God would have plans for us to meet again. Little did I know the great purpose and assignment that would be a part of the God-design of my life and work. Remember my family tree project? A seed was planted for my "tree" of life to expand and grow.

Being married, having my daughter (another story), and eventually divorced, God continued to work on me and my feelings of family and healing. I was still seeking where God wanted me, so I chose early in my career to align and work with children needing emotional and behavioral support. Later, I added all young children with any developmental or special needs to have therapeutic and educational support along with their families. I loved my work, and my healing continued with my children. God was showing me the way!

Every believer has received "grace gifts," so use them to serve one another as faithful stewards of the many colored tapestries of God's grace:

> "Above all, constantly echo God's intense love for one another, for love will be a canopy over many sins" (wrongdoings). 1 Peter 4:8 The Passion Translation

God commanded me to come to Texas when I was 39 years old. I was alone, divorced, and away from all my family and friends. My job was a new dream for me at another university. After arriving, I felt the desolation of my life. The abandonment feelings crept in, and I prayed to return home to Florida many times. Why would God bring me to this strange new place and forget about me? Through my prayers, I found friends, a church family who accepted me with open arms, and my forever family in my husband, Art. He welcomed my mom and daughter into our family tree… forever growing and expanding its roots and branch outreaching with love, acceptance, and direction. He brought back feelings I had experienced with my dad, and we created a relationship of God's love and healing between us.

Art and I began growing our roots and intertwined into my tree through his young adult kids, Luke and Heather while welcoming my daughter and granddaughter, Maggie and Catie. The roots continued with our elderly moms, his brothers and sisters, and extended family.

As our children became adults and began growing in their trees of life, we grew exponentially and covered the land. Marriages and grandchildren entered our life… however they came to us… step-children, step-grandchildren, adopted "kids," and adults needing love and family… our hearts expanded, and our trees grew, budded, and blossomed. The lessons of love, loss, communication, and acceptance consistently brought us seasons of growth in our own lives.

God shows us how we can bring His Love into the lives of others through His anointed, supernatural, and blessed Word.

Just a few years ago during the COVID years, my daughter had been using her time being housebound to research our family tree, our biological one. Only knowing the basics about my past was challenging for her. During my first and only call with my sister, I tried desperately to soak up any information, reasoning, connection, and love I could. I knew she was doing the same. There was a phrase my sister said that stayed with me for years. While seeking to find her again, praying and asking God for her to come back into my life at the right time, I held on to this simple statement, "I KNEW we would be amazing friends if we were in each other's life." Little did I know, she would return at just the right time. That IS how God creates His perfect plan: the perfect timing, way, and outcome for HEALING.

Maybe I should let HER tell you... meet my "Irish Twin" sister, Pastor Jody Glass!

> Years ago, my mother came to my house on the east coast of Florida and sat down and told me that when I was 13 months old, she gave birth to a baby girl, my sister. She intended to raise us together. Unfortunately, our father had a messy divorce and wanted to marry our mother as soon as possible. But because of many complicated issues at the time, my mother was forced to decide to give the baby girl up for adoption. My parents did eventually marry and tried to reverse the adoption. But it was too late. This caused my mother much pain throughout the years. This explained a lot of things in my growing up. As she told me the whole story, it was disturbing and made me angry. I looked at my mother and said to her, "You know what I'm going to do? I'm going to find her!"
>
> She said she knew I would want to do that and would help me. So I hired a private investigator, and in about two weeks, I heard back that she had found my sister.
>
> I called the number given to me and got to talk to her for a while. But it was not a good time for us to be a part of each other's lives, Even though it was what we both wanted. So in the next few years, we separately moved away from Florida to other states and lost track of each other.

I prayed that, at some point, the Lord would bring her back into my life. I knew the timing of the Lord was perfect. So when I opened a Facebook account, I would search for her occasionally. But with no idea of her married name or where she lived, it was a shot in the dark with no results. So I just kept trusting God and praying for her.

Then one evening in June, after my birthday, I received a message from a young woman [my daughter] that asked me if I was the Jody Glass, that might have had a younger sister that had been given up for adoption. I was so excited. I turned to my husband and gave him my phone to read the message!

We got to talk for the first time in over 30 years, and it was the perfect timing. We have an ongoing conversation as sisters do. The parallels in our lives are remarkable! We both had just written and published a book just before we connected. We both minister to others. I am a pastor and have Legacy Bible School. Her publishing company is Legacy, also. There are many more unusual similarities that we share. But the love we have for each other is extraordinary and unique.

The Lord knew when and why we needed to connect and be a part of each other's lives. I am so thankful to Him for His ways and timing. Finally, finally, I have my sister back!!

(Thanks, sis, I love you!)

What a whirlwind life can be! Yet, God is always good through it all! That is His promise to us. When others close a door or restrict us, God finds a way to bring us exactly what we need.

Can I tell you I am completely healed from abandonment, aloneness, approval-seeking, and other moments that occurred in my life when grief, loss, doubt, and pain were present?

I CAN tell you this, I am a work in progress as I follow Christ, and he continues to unlock and heal every crevice I have closed tightly. God heals us completely! I have honed numerous Grace Gifts for God and use them in my practice and outreach with others. They are always a work in progress, too. I am part of God's Army to reveal and enhance the Kingdom of God on this earth. I am a leader in this "movement," and my tribe of individuals around me is healing their own life's purpose path. We are all accepted and re-born into the Family of God. Won't you join us? YOU are now part of my TREE! Welcome!

Reflection

constantly echo Gods intense love for one another

1 Peter 4:8

extra-ordinary kingdom ambassadors

Activating Your Spiritual Senses to His World

Kim Vastine

"We are ambassadors of the Anointed One who carry the message of Christ to the world, as though God were tenderly pleading with them directly through our lips. So, we tenderly plead with you on Christ's behalf, turn back to God and be reconciled to him." 2 Corinthians 5:20

"Open your mouth and taste. Open your eyes and see—how good God is. Blessed are you who run to him." Psalm 34:8

Wherever you go in the world, you can joyfully observe children in playtime, acting out roles of imagination. They are teachers, firemen, magicians, astronauts, doctors, etc. It's fun to ask them at different stages of life what they want to be when they grow up. It is still one of the first questions we ask when being introduced to one another in formal or informal settings. We often discuss a person's title and who they are when introducing them at a party or event. But the big question is always: Who are you, and what do you do?

I do not remember much play or dream time as a child. My family circumstances required me to care for my siblings while my parents were at work. In those days and cultures, it was common for children to be seen and not heard in families. However, my mother faithfully took us to church several times a week. There I met Jesus and found the only safe place to discover expression for my voice and who I wanted to be.

I explored and experienced great joy through my voice by singing worship songs. Heartfelt melodies flowed through my vocal cords as though I was flinging open wide the window of my soul. One Saturday morning, my mom was ironing clothes in the garage when she encouraged me to sing with her. The acoustics in our garage magnified our voices as we sang out in a duet, "It is no secret what God can do, what He's done for others, He'll do for you." The following day at Sunday morning service, she was asked by the pastor to come up near the piano to sing a solo for the congregation worship time. She quickly motioned for me to come up and join her in singing that same wonderful song together. I found my forever-precious space with Jesus at that moment. My heartfelt song connected permanently to His heart like a little song sparrow bird.

I surrendered my heart to Jesus Christ and was baptized at around eight. I had such a remarkable and powerful sense of knowing that He saw, understood, and loved me. Tears poured down my face like a river on that day of encountering Him. I began singing solos around that time, and it became my daydream to be a powerful worship singer, directing choirs and creating atmospheres so that when people would engage, they would feel God's presence deeply. They would surrender and magnify Him wholeheartedly, just as I did. God's presence was so tangible to me as a child. To this day, I live life experiencing and enjoying His shining face, which is more magnified when I sing to Him. My heart explodes with joy in those times when I hear Him sing over me, as well. You and I have been invited into an epic divine romance for eternity.

Psalm 34:8, "Open your mouth and taste, open your eyes and see—how good God is. Blessed are you who run to him." Our incredible Creator designed us to understand and perceive the world around us with our five senses: taste, smell, touch, hearing, and sight. Those senses can be beautiful, practical, and enjoyed, but they can also be critical pain points that linger in the photo album of our memories.

Some of my weekdays consisted of skipping into the house after school to smell my grandma's freshly baked cinnamon rolls, anticipating those buttery pieces melting in my mouth. When freshly bathed on Saturday nights, my mom would wash, comb, and carefully roll my hair in pink sponge rollers to have perfect ringlets for Sunday school the next day.

On the other side of those sensations was the brutal shock of physical pain in private places in my body that felt foreign and somehow shameful, hearing frightful screams from death threats issued by my birth father, watching violent acts in our home that would bring fearful paralysis. For many years, all those memories, along with my physical, mental, and emotional senses, were operating in a mode of trauma I did not fully recognize or understand.

My parents divorced when I was eleven years old. Life became very different after that when a few years later, my mom remarried a good man who helped rebuild our family. Following High School, I went to Bible College, where I met the man I eventually married. Life moved along quickly, and in time we had two exceptional children. I worked in the corporate business arena and continued with music ministry in various churches.

Each year it seemed the pressing demands of life revealed more significant pockets of pain and behaviors that I could no longer ignore. Deep, recognizable soul pain would fiercely demand a reckoning that took me on a dive into Scripture, prayer, spiritual healing books, research, and counseling to acknowledge the secrets of my childhood to heal. I was challenged and encouraged by the journey of refusing to be a victim of past circumstances. It was a treasure hunt of discovery to learn that wholeness in Him would only come through endless daily choices to live purposefully with profound gratitude for every trial, betrayal, wound, opportunity, and aspect of goodness given to me in life.

Someone wise said, "What we are is God's gift to us, but what we become is our gift to Him." Those life challenges helped me become strong and resilient. They gave enormous empathy for others who had experienced trauma. As I began to heal, I could often recognize and spiritually see people's pain. I began to speak and minister in groups sharing the message of hope for others to confront the secrets that were infecting their souls and receive the freedom that was theirs in Christ alone. It was liberating to see people freed from the prison of their pasts.

In 2002, while serving as a Worship Pastor, I was asked to preach my first message in the pulpit at the weekend services. After ministering at all the benefits that weekend, I was somewhat surprised to learn that one of the women in the congregation decided to leave the church out of an offense that a woman was preaching in the pulpit. I had already found that being a woman in ministry was often challenging. Who am I, was the question I constantly queried before the Lord. It was a familiar question I had asked in previous years when ministry functions or jobs would end or my role would significantly change.

That led me into a tough, challenging season of rediscovering who I was in Christ alone. It needed to matter more what He said about me than anyone else. I had a fresh new awakening during prayer and meditation that was later encouraged by spiritual brothers and sisters. Excitedly, the vision came about to launch a non-profit ministry called Ambassador Alliance International. These Scriptures became a roadmap message, John 14:12a "The person who follows me in faith, believing in me, will do the same mighty miracles that I do—even greater miracles than these…" and 2 Corinthians 5:20, "We are ambassadors of the Anointed One who carry the message of Christ to the world, as though God were tenderly pleading with them directly through our lips. So we tenderly plead with you on Christ's behalf, 'Turn back to God and be reconciled to him.'"

Warning! This kind of living is simple but costly to your comfort zone.

Miraculous opportunities came to teach, minister, pray and bring His healing power into Egypt, Africa, India, South America, the U.S., and beyond. My message was the same whether it was to the widow in the thatched hut in a remote village in Kenya, illiterate women or orphans in India, or the youth in the deserts of Egypt. YOU matter to God's heart, and your life has a divine purpose! When you belong to Him, you become His mouthpiece and an ambassador, a diplomat of heaven, with legal authority from the Holy Spirit to be His representative wherever you go. His power has given you everything needed to change the world around you, starting with the one right before you. You start by opening your hand to share His story in your life, your bread with the hungry little ones running around the village, inviting someone to your kitchen table, and watch how God will supply more because it is His job to do the multiplication. Then, he looks for a willing heart to say, "Yes, Lord, what can I do?"

We carried practical life-giving supplies to orphans and widows. We ministered to abused, often illiterate women in India and saw them set free as they received Jesus as their Savior and Liberator. They experienced with their physical senses the goodness of God in the practical items we carried to them. They also felt the tangible presence of God in times of ministry, teaching, and prayer as "the eyes of their heart" were opened.

We later heard many ongoing reports as their regenerated hearts began to bring change in their marriages, families, and villages, on the streets of Cairo and in the orphanages of Kenya and India. We challenged each one to go and do likewise and give it away and see what God would do in it. Their stories have changed my life forever.

One of the women we ministered to in Kenya was praying about starting an orphanage. We encouraged her to start with what she had and see how God would multiply. Today, my friend, Flora Mwakali, has New Scent School near Nairobi, Kenya, where abandoned and horrifically abused girls can come to live, find refuge, schooling, and future hope. She works with few resources but emphatically states, "I could not continue to look the other way and ignore the similar plight of my little sisters." She is living a very sacrificial life today and finding great joy in bringing liberation and freedom to more than 50 young girls that now have a home with daily food, clothing/shoes, academic education, and spiritual healing. She teaches them to forgive their offenders, and they will find the freedom that only Jesus Christ offers. She is living by the Golden Rule every day that beautifully proclaims to the world, "Love others the way you want to be loved."

Anita Scott, our God-daughter, lived in an area of the city that many would consider to be a socio-economically depressed area. She discovered young kids wandering aimlessly around the complex after school and began building relationships with them. After-school snacks became the magnet that drew them to come to Bible studies that she began having. She would listen

"God's creative life in me multiplies abundance to give others."

Kim Vastine

to their harrowing stories about life, teach them to pray and listen to His voice. Single moms started reaching out for help, families needed food and support, and the list of needs began growing. As part of Anita's spiritual community, we prayed and started a simple gathering in her living room to share the good news of Jesus Christ to satisfy their hungry hearts. We provided childcare and took up a collection to help pay rent for a single mom who would be evicted. The apartment swimming pool became the new baptismal area. Before long, Anita was training the residents to care for each other and meet the needs that were arising daily. The joy around the community was so remarkable that the apartment management was effusive in their gratitude for the changes they could see happening. Anita became a Kingdom of Heaven ambassador and trained and raised even the youngest of people to understand the rule of heaven that it is "more blessed to give than receive."

Cassidy Littleton, another beautiful God-daughter, experienced part of her life in foster care. Today, at 24 years old, she advocates for those in the foster care system. She is passionate about changing a legal system that often forgets these children of God. Her fiery passion represents Jesus' love and nurturing in many seen and unseen ways. She has learned to embrace the pain of her past and bring healing to others. She knows who she is in Christ Jesus and walks with admirable confidence and humility in the opportunities she has been given to speak up on this issue throughout the United States.

Laurel Wheeler is a young beautiful college graduate who is physically blind. She relies heavily on her other physical and spiritual senses to navigate life. Yet, she has a heart like Jesus, full of compassion for visually impaired individuals in other countries with little to no resources. So, she created a nonprofit called www.LaurelWheelerFoundation.org which provides international relief for the blind and visually impaired through technology, training tools, and other resources. Her motto is "The only thing you need to change a person's life is a willing heart!"

I stopped in for a quick lunch at a restaurant on a hectic day. Hurrying through the line to place my order, it was clear the lady serving behind the counter was not happy to be working. As I went to sit at my table, I could hear the Holy Spirit whisper to my heart to go and share a simple word of encouragement with her. When finding her, I privately and quietly shared that God wanted me to tell her that He really saw her and loved her so much. He knew she felt like He'd forgotten her and didn't care that she was struggling and felt so alone. I then slipped a $20 bill in her hand as a token that God saw her needs and would take care of her. She began sobbing as she ran around the counter to grab me in a bear hug and, in a different voice, exclaimed, "Oh, how could you possibly know this? You have no idea what this means to me. I've just about given up on God. I thought He didn't care about me anymore. But, you've given me hope today." I almost missed a holy moment that day.

"Simple acts of love can light up a heart with hope."

These days, you can find me working as a REALTOR® here in the Dallas/Fort Worth area, helping individuals and families navigate life changes in buying and selling their homes. I am constantly in prayer about how to best represent Jesus as I serve them with professional excellence and, most importantly, His love and care. On other days, I counsel hurting hearts, facilitate a church gathering, serve at the homeless center, pray at a City Council meeting, or have lunch with a neighbor.

Whether I am selling real estate, ministering and teaching in a special gathering here locally or in the city of Gulu, Uganda, the people in my neighborhood, the business marketplace, or event platforms are all important to Him.

May you and I choose to be His ambassador in our world daily, loving others with His senses operating in you through the Holy Spirit. Represent Jesus in who you are. Be His goodness that heals, restores, sees, and gives a voice to those without a voice.

Tag! You're it!

Reflection

closing

The Great Commission

Lori L. Dixon, Ed.S.

You've been called to action! It is YOUR time! We need your purpose and your mission right now. Your assignment is unique to you. God placed it within you when you left Heaven to reside in your small Earthly body. It was a seed put deep in your soul to activate at just the right time. That time is your calling, and YOU will know when you feel God's nudging to awaken and walk in it.

> Then Jesus came close to them and said, "All authority of the universe has been given to me. Now wherever you go, make disciples of all nations, baptizing them in the name of the Father, the Son, and the Holy Spirit. And teach them to faithfully

follow all that I have commanded you. And never forget that I am with you every day, even to the completion of this age."
—The Great Commission from Jesus in Matthew 28:18-20

Do you feel it? The calling in your soul?

How will you respond?

Will you answer, "Yes, Lord," or say, "I'm not ready?"

Jesus commissioned us all who follow him. As his followers, we are commanded to walk in HIS wisdom and be ready for the journey ahead with him leading...." I am with you every day, even to the completion of this age." What a promise.

Now I ask you, will you accept?

> "Never doubt God's mighty power to work in you and accomplish all this. He will achieve infinitely more than your most significant request, your most unbelievable dream, and exceed your wildest imagination! He will outdo them all, for his miraculous power constantly energizes you. Now we offer to God all the glorious praise that rises from every church in every generation through Jesus Christ—and all that will yet be manifest through time and eternity! Amen!" Ephesians 3:20-21 The Passion Translation

We welcome YOU! We embrace YOU! We hope this book has been a blessing to you and that you will consider joining us, your sisters in Christ. Thank you for choosing to read and be part of...

Revealing the Wisdom on the Walk

allison byrd-haley
intentional

Allison Byrd-Haley is a native Texan. Allison's caring nature through her childhood led her into healthcare in 1998, when her second child was diagnosed with cancer, she used all her love, faith, strength and knowledge to take care of him. By the grace of God, he recovered and for 10 years she raised her two children as a single parent, until she met her wonderful husband. In 2011, Allison's mom was given the awful news that she had terminal cancer, and for the 3 months of treatment, Allison went to every appointment to make sure her mother got the best care. Allison was determined after her passing to always do something to give back. A few years later, she started her nonprofit, Heavenly Mimi. Having an organization that can bless others is one of her purposed in life. Allison believes that we have one life and all of us need to make a difference.

Email: abhaley1975@gmail.com

IG: @allison_byrd_haley

becky dozeman
MSW, LMSW

surrender

Becky is a graduate of Calvin University and The University of Michigan with a Master of Social Work degree. Becky has spent the past 2 decades serving as a helping professional. She is a licensed clinical/macro social worker, therapist, and wellness life coach. In 2021 she took a leap into entrepreneurship launching Her Best Yes Counseling & Coaching Services. A decision made following God's call on her life to empower Christian women to lean into who God has created them to be. She is passionate about helping women integrate spiritual, mental, emotional, physical, and relational health into daily life. Becky serves women through individual counseling/coaching, speaking, retreats, events, and group programs to uncover their best yeses for a thriving life. She supports imperfect women who are showing up during the challenges of life, in order for them to live bravely, improve hope-filled thinking, and decrease mental clutter so that they can compassionately show up in their lives like never before. She loves traveling, staying active, reading, spending time outdoors, family movie nights, & laughter:) She lives in Michigan with her husband Jason, son Drake, daughter Charlotte, and their chocolate lab.

FB: Becky Dozeman

IG: herbestyes

becky@herbestyes.com

Website: herbestyes.com

deanna blair

warrior

Deanna is a Mental Health & Toxicity speaker, Ozone Therapist and Detox specialist with Core Frequency Therapy. Deanna began writing almost 9 years ago after she got out of a mentally abusive relationship. She has a passion for running and while out one day she was pondering the challenging year, pulled out her phone and began writing beautiful words of healing and encouragement that she felt coming from the Lord. The words were incredible and she was hooked on writing. She stopped writing for a while but when her mom got sick about five years ago, she picked it up again. This started her on a new journey with her business, Core Frequency Therapy and speaking on Mental Health and toxicity. It has also helped renew the relationship with her mom and a much stronger relationship with God.

Email: Spotthedots12@gmail.com   IG: CoreFrequencyTherapyLLC

FB: CoreFrequencyTherapyLLC   Twitter: SpotTheDots12

irum rashid-jones

shine

Irum is a woman of many hats. She's a mom, wife, trusted advisor, award-winning business coach, entrepreneur, author, podcaster, & philanthropist! The gift she shares with the world is her ability to transform communities & businesses into functioning & flourishing environments. In addition to this hard work, her heart work is education, family values & creating opportunities. As a highly sought-after advisor to over 100 global non-profits, she currently serves as the President of Dallas Professional Women; a network of women on a mission to create a better tomorrow by leading professional training, coaching & brand extension solutions. She also serves over 80K entrepreneurs & professionals across different industries and verticals including non-profits helping to reach their goals! Irum is the brains behind cultivating and nurturing 1M+ online members on social media. She has a winning track record of positioning critical & key communications to help extend brand identity. Irum also believes in giving back and has been involved in various philanthropic ventures including working with refugees and promoting education for under-resourced communities.

Email: Irum.jones@gmail.com
Website: www.electricianoncall.com
IG: ladypro_irumjones
FB: irum.jones

jackie davis
rooted

A strong advocate for women, Jackie Davis has dedicated her life to empowering women from all walks of life. Revered among her peers as a world visionary leader who offers coaching for women to reach their God-given purpose and goals through mentoring and ministry. Jackie was in the medical field for 35 years, including owning and operating multiple Medical Spas throughout the Dallas area. She soon plunged into obtaining her certification as a Life Coach and combined her experience as a Women's bible group leader to better serve her women-based clientele. One of the many things Jackie encountered while mentoring women is their desire to find authentic, meaningful friendships with other women. Jackie had the vision for the Pinky Swear Mission and began hosting the Pinky Swear radio talk show. Jackie has a creative side that is expressed through interior design through her personal venture known as Fancy Fleur Boutique. One of Jackie's "Golden rules" is *"Be blessed and be a Blessing."* Most recently, Jackie and her husband built their dream home in Oklahoma. She hopes to spend days in her vegetable and flower garden, as well as learn beekeeping. But most of all spending time with her husband, adult children, grandchildren and serving the Lord.

Email: jackelyndavis@gmail.com   IG: @Jackie_s._davis

judy cochrane
love

Over the years, Judy Cochrane sought to unveil grace where there was grit. That led her to her faith where she would seek greater understanding of God, self, others and circumstance. She now holds numerous certifications in various mental & emotional health modalities: Hypnotherapy, Neuro Linguistic Practitioner (NLP), Yoga Teacher, Energetic Healing Arts, Meditation facilitator and others…that have to do with God, art, music & believing there is good in the world. Cochrane is a multi-passionate entrepreneur. She is an Author of two books*, Founder & CEO of R. House Publishing, a Book Coach, a Ghostwriter, a Wellness Coach, Owner of AWAREHOUSE [merch. lifestyle. wellness] Offering online products for inspired living (apparel, jewelry, wall art, home, & self-help tools.) She's the creator of spiritualit**ee** (pronounced: spirituality) which is an inspirational clothing and jewelry line (wholesale/retail). She also designs lines of products for other authors, speakers and churches. Her inspirational products, tees and books can be found on her website.

Email: hello@jccochrane.com

Website: www.jccochrane.com or www.awarehouse.life

kim vastine

soar

Kim has been a passionate lover, worshipper and follower of Jesus Christ for much of her life. Involved in various facets of ministry in founding an international non-profit ministry organization, serving as a worship pastor in the D/FW area of Texas, along with Chaplaincy, Life Coaching and planting house churches. Her organization Ambassador Alliance International was privileged to train, encourage and support marginalized women and orphanages. With 20+ years in the business marketplace and corporate arena, she teaches and believes the Kingdom of God should be fully expressed by all believers 24/7 days a week, in the marketplace, for city, national and international transformation. She currently serves as a Real Estate Professional in the state of Texas. Serves on the international board of directors for World Embrace in Uganda and Threshing Floor Ministries, a local Dallas ministry to the homeless and solitary who God loves to "bring into family". She's received an honorary doctorate degree for her life work and enjoys being a designated *International Golden Rule Ambassador*. She and her husband live in Texas and have two married adult children and two wonderful grand-joys that light up her life! She's blessed to have many adopted, spiritual sons and daughters all over the globe.

kim@kimvastine.com   IG : @ksv0718

FB: @kim.vastine   Website: AnchorHomeTeam.com

krista medlock

connect

Krista Medlock's personal mantra, "It's kind of fun to do the impossible", is the daily "grit" check that she uses in her personal and professional pursuits. As the owner of a strategic consultancy and the coveted company, The Girl Cave, Krista is a visionary that believes she can change the world. She is a former Miss Richardson, Miss Highland Park USA, and Miss Lake Highlands USA with appearances on Good Morning Texas, International Beauty Shows, and notable podcasts. Through speaking, Krista uses her life experiences to inspire and activate purpose and potential. When she is not facing life head-on, she is watching a good Lifetime Movie, traveling, or enjoying a meal with her friends.

Email : krista@kristamedlock.com

IG: @krista_medlock

FB: krista.medlock

lulite ejigu
glory

Lulite Ejigu runs a consulting and management firm, mostly serving as a Senior Advisor to large-scale corporations & institutions in both the public and private sectors globally. Prior to consulting, she served as an Executive Director at J.P. Morgan Chase & Co. and has extensive years of experience in the financial industry. Lulite has been recognized for her Leadership in Dallas, New York, Washington D.C., and Addis Ababa, Ethiopia. She is a tactical innovator who enjoys finding solutions to close the gap between the unbanked and unhoused, who may not be digitally and/or financially literate, by helping people and institutions expand their impact and network. Lulite's focus on social justice investment is reflected in her track record of championing programs that aid the disadvantaged as part of a Triple Bottom Line approach to business. Lulite holds an Executive MBA from Texas A&M University-Commerce with a concentration in Global Operations & Strategic Management and a BA in Psychology and Communication Studies from Texas Tech University. Outside of work, Lulite remains an active problem solver, always looking for solutions to address issues raised in the communities she is a part of and beyond. Lulite also enjoys hiking and experiencing new cultures by traveling abroad with friends and family.

Email : mailto:lulite.ejigu@gmail.com   IG: @lulite

Twitter: @lulite_ejigu

molly brown
faithfulness

Molly Brown is a born and raised Wisconsin girl. After college, given her adventurous nature, she thought it would be "fun" to move to Texas for a year. 16 years later, she is now considered a Texan. Molly initially taught Spanish for several years. After battling and defeating stage 4 cancer, she was called to serve students and families in public education through school counseling. She earned a Master's of Education from Dallas Baptist University. The past 4 years has brought a season of complete transformation in just about every area of life. God is revealing incredible plans for her future including writing, speaking, and professionally counseling. She recently began further coursework to pursue a license in Professional Counseling. Molly is passionate about walking with others through life's seasons, and by sharing her testimony and God-given wisdom, she encourages others with God's hope and future. She is active as a yoga instructor at Sanara Yoga & Wellness in Southlake, Texas. She is a runner, slowly training for her 7th marathon. Day to day, she loves reading, watching most sports (Go Pack Go!), gardening, cooking, and taking walks around my neighborhood in Grapevine, Texas with my spunky sidekick, an English bulldog named Maggie.

Email: mmbrown262@gmail.com   IG: @mmbrown262

shae stewart

seek

Meet the author and Lead Editor of this book, Shae Stewart. Shae is Momma to her three grown children and their spouses, Honey to three grandchildren, Lovie to her husband, and MamaShae to many friends. Shae recently gained three bonus sons when she married the man who was her best friend for nearly four decades. She holds many titles, not only in her personal life but also in her professional life. With over 25 years and several different roles in the health insurance industry, Shae has always enjoyed building successful organizations from the ground up, promoting operational and strategic efficiencies. As a self-proclaimed "old soul" and empath, Shae adores (most) people and strives to help those in need, whether that means anonymously buying someone a meal, praying for any and every person she possibly can, or lending a shoulder to struggling friends, family, or even strangers. She is a world traveler and lover of life, and many call Shae and her husband "funhavers." Despite living a life filled with the losses of many close to her, Shae finds peace, understanding, strength, spirituality, and hope through The Father, His perfect Son, Jesus, and Holy Spirit.

Email: shaeluca@gmail.com   IG: mamashaeluca

FB: Shae.Lucabaugh

stephanie vasquez

growth

Stephanie is first the daughter of the King. Single mother of 3, entrepreneur. She's an artist and lover of art. She has a heart for others and loves helping people. She's an inventor, resourceful, and adventurous.

Email: vasquez.stephaniej@gmail.com

IG: @love_on_a_loop

FB: stephanie.vasquez.564

meet Lori L. Dixon

@walkwithlori
@lorilanedixon

Lori L. Dixon, Ed.S. is a Visionary and Epiphany Expert with her business ventures, LLD Legacy Media and Publishing, Walk with Lori, and LLD Legacy. Lori brings more than 4 decades of wisdom and experience working in education, therapies, business, and nonprofits. She is a best-selling author and publisher, as well as a multiple international award-winning host and producer on streaming TV. With her dynamic television appearances on Bravo's Real Housewives of Dallas, Lori understands the 'reality' of how the next chapter of life may be rewritten at any time. She may be now watched internationally on TV as a co-host on Lite It Up TV and Sawubona...I SEE You on ZondraTV Network on ROKU, AmazonFire, Chromecast, and iTunes.

Lori believes in finding the "heartstrings" in life, releasing the strongholds of fear, and living the life God has designed for you. As a writer for many years and a published author, editor, and frequent media influencer for others, Lori knew her passion would always be in the "stories" of our lives. She expanded her mission to publishing with anthologies, compilations, and children's books. Lori believes we are all SEEN in our own God-given divine design and that we have a mission to share it right now within the world.

Through LLD Legacy Media and Publishing, which is a full-service publishing company with editing, writing, illustrating, design, media, and marketing, she brings her passions together for each author. Her newest program, Wisdom on the Walk (WoW) is a unique Anthology PLUS Journey for women to become authors and further their own stories and missions for others.

Walk with Lori
VISIONARY LEADER

LORI L. DIXON, Ed.S.
Founder and Owner, LLD Legacy and Walk with Lori
TheraCoach, Publisher
International Multiple Award-Winning Host and Producer

469-855-0287
www.walkwithlori.com
lori@walkwithlori.com

Wisdom on the Walk (WoW) Unique Anthology PLUS book!

Spirit-filled, God-directed, Purpose-driven Life Stories

Has God specifically chosen YOU to be part of a new project to bring forth God's purpose in our lives? YOU are invited to be one of twelve women sharing stories in this meaningful anthology. It is more than a book; it is an interactive journey of reflection, creativity, learning, connecting, and revealing God's work in your life to influence and impact others. That is why we call it an **Anthology PLUS** book. Your story will be intertwined with the writing of Lori L. Dixon, drawings by a local artist, and graphic designs to engage you in furthering your purpose.

I love how God designed that we would have 12! What a beautiful and meaningful way to further HIS Kingdom by creating circles of disciples for unique and powerful purposes. We will spend much time together, sharing information, stories, insights, support, faith, and growth moments.

Welcome to the Wisdom on the Walk Author Journey!

Here are some quick items to know about the experience:

- We meet monthly for 6-7 months.
- Each session includes mentoring, learning, connection, interaction with other authors, bible study, and prayer.
- You will also have a 1:1 session each month for guidance and direction in your writing, faith walk, social media presence, marketing, media, and more!
- Our upcoming retreat in Dallas is in July for sharing, mentoring, and speaking.
- The next sister circle of 12 will begin in August. That's how Jesus rippled God's word!

Meet our LLD Legacy Publishing and Media Team:

Lori Dixon
owner, author, and your visionary leader in the process

Shae Lucabaugh
author and editor

Jordan Mitchell
virtual assistant and support

Callie Revell
graphic design, support, and social media

We ARE also looking for new authors for women, children, or other anthologies!

Do you hear that? A call to action. Are you feeling your name among the 12? Have you ever thought God wants you to share your life story, healing, transformation, and insights with other women and glorify His work in YOU?

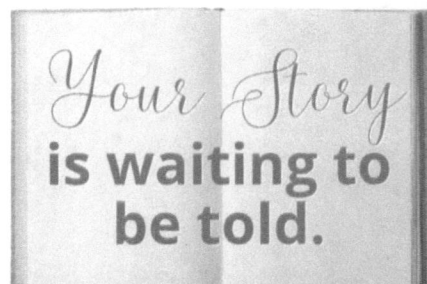

Contact us for more information about the WoW Journey or to publish your book with us!

Did you gain wisdom on your walk?
Order more copies to pour into others!

www.walkwithlori.com/wisdomonwalk

or scan this code with your phone:

www.ingramcontent.com/pod-product-compliance
Lightning Source LLC
Chambersburg PA
CBHW020516080526
44583CB00013B/624